India as an IT Superpower

The Strategy for Success

Anurag Sharma

Dedicated to two wonderful people
Shrimati Rama Devi and Shri Ghanshyam Sharma
Who happen to be my parents too

Acknowledgements

This book was not possible without the inspiration and continuous support of Dr. Umarani Pappuswamy, and Mr. Ravi Dutt Sharma.

INDIA AS AN IT SUPERPOWER

The Strategy for Success

By

Anurag Sharma

Preface

India's dramatic growth of the IT industry over the last couple of decades has made news all over the world. The incarnation of an impoverished developing country into a leader of Information Technology (IT) has surprised the scholars and the common folk alike. What helped the transition of an over populous country dealing with problems of illiteracy and malnutrition, natural disasters like draught, floods, earthquakes and tsunami besides terrorism and five full blown wars since independence into a situation where it is excelling in the cutting edge areas of IT and knowledge management?

Is India's growth in Information technology a reality or hype? Is it a bubble ready to get busted? Is it just coincidental? Is it really a historical accident? Is it a direct result of the liberalization process? Didn't it start before liberalization? Is this success superficial or deep-rooted inside Indian culture? What unique factors helped India move from a third world country to an Information superpower? Is this success sustainable and long lasting?

Conventional explanations seem incomplete or unsatisfactory. Going beyond the obvious, this research explores the issue with a difference. This book examines the challenges and ascertains their gravity. It also explores and explains unique inherent strengths of India. It investigates the role of the government policies in India's advent as an IT superpower. Finally, this research presents the India Information Technology Success (IITS) model. The IITS model explains why Indian success is sustainable. IITS model can help other countries effectively emulate India's success.

India as an IT Superpower
The Strategy for Success
By
Anurag Sharma

Shashwat Books
* Bareilly * Delhi * Pittsburgh *

© 2007-2009 by Anurag Sharma.

The author would be pleased to receive email correspondence regarding this publication or related topics at indiasmart@gmail.com.

ISBN-13 (paperback): 978-1-44865-199-3
ISBN-10 (paperback): 1-44865-199-9

Printed and bound in the United States of America.

Trademarked names may appear in this book. Rather than use a trademark symbol with every occurrence of a trademarked name, we use the names only in an editorial fashion and to the benefit of the trademark owner, with no intention of infringement of the trademark.

Distributed to the book trade worldwide by Shashwat Books, Pittsburgh (USA), e-mail orders-indiasmart@gmail.com, or visit http://www.smartindian.com/it-super-power.htm.

For information on translations, please contact the author at 9324 Aldenford Drive, Pittsburgh, PA 15237, e-mail anurag@hitechclub.com, or visit http://www.smartindian.com/it-super-power.htm.

The information in this book is distributed on an "as is" basis, without warranty. All URLs have been verified at the time of publication, but we take no responsibility for what has happened since. Although every precaution has been taken in the preparation of this work, neither the author nor the publisher shall have any liability to any person or entity with respect to any loss or damage caused or alleged to be caused directly or indirectly by the information contained in this work.

Table of Contents

INTRODUCTION

1.1. Aims and Objectives of the Study

Information technology (IT) is a globally competitive and highly advanced industry. When a so called third world country shows major gains in IT and other advanced technologies, it surprises the world. The software industry in India gained recognition in the early eighties when a handful of companies took up export of trained software manpower, especially to USA. Soon, Indian companies and professionals acquired an important place in global IT scenario. This was unprecedented when a country jumped from agrarian economy to knowledge economy bypassing the industrial revolution completely. Experts are busy today to explain the trends and circumstances behind this success. Due to the stereotyping, not many scholars, economists or industry experts could foresee or predict India's success in an advanced area until it really happened.

This book explores the key success factors of and the challenges before Indian IT sector despite of much theoretical impossibility. It evaluates India's success in IT and tests if the success is sustainable. It analyzes the role of the government policies in making this success a reality. It tests the relevant theories and existing models and explores the possibility of developing a model of success of Indian IT industry which can be adopted by other countries to achieve similar success in IT or other areas.

1.2. Research Questions

This book seeks answers to the following questions:

- Is India really shining in IT?
- What are the contributing factors to India's success in IT?
- Did Indian culture help or hinder the success?
- What makes Indian IT companies competitive and efficient?
- What role did Government policies play in India's success in IT?
- Do existing theories explain India's success in IT?
- Is it possible to develop a model from this success?

- Is this success sustainable?
- Can this success model be imitated by other industries and other nations?

1.3. Research Methodologies, Tools and Techniques

This research evaluates Indian IT's case with the help of existing theories and secondary data available from various sources including research papers, dissertations, interviews, books, articles and official releases. It explores the Success Factors for Indian IT. It also analyses some existing models while assessing the strengths and weaknesses of Indian IT industry. A short survey (see Appendix A) of 20 software professionals from India and the USA is also used to guide the direction of the research.

1.4. Significance of the Study

This research is an explorative journey with an aim to create a model for India's success in IT sector. This model will help in achieving similar success in other sectors. The same model may help other countries identifying their strengths in IT, Knowledge Management (KM) and other highly advanced technological areas.

1.5. Scope and Limitations of the Study

IT in general refers to the digital processing, storage and communication of information of all kinds and design and development of software and hardware used or developed for this purpose. Throughout this dissertation, the term IT is used to include software and software enabled services, and Business Process Outsourcing (BPO) segment. Though, it may cover hardware at times but in general, the hardware design and development is outside the purview of this dissertation. Also, the communication segments of the ICT sector such as conventional telecommunications or mobile telephony are not covered in this dissertation.

1.6. Organization of the Chapters

The book is divided into 8 chapters. Following the introduction in this chapter, the remaining components of this book are described below briefly.

Chapter 2 presents an overview of India in Information Age. It provides background information on India especially the history of information, IT and computing. It also has a passing reference to the state of other hi-tech areas.

Chapter 3 reviews key indicators and facts to ensure that India's success is not just hype.

Chapter 4 focuses on the challenges India had to face throughout the process in order to succeed in its IT industry. This chapter classifies the threats into three categories depending on their level.

Chapter 5 describes the major Success Factors that were vital in the success. It presents these factors in a systematic way and highlights the most important ones that need to be paid special attention to. It emphasises the need to analyse government policies in a separate chapter.

Chapter 6 examines how Government Policies affected the success of the IT industry. Light is thrown on the policies such as education which have a tremendous though indirect effect on IT industry.

Chapter 7 analyses existing theories and models in context of the Indian IT industry and develops a new model called Indian IT Success (IITS) model. It also successfully tests if IITS model can be used by other industries or countries.

Chapter 8 covers discussion and conclusions.

Besides the above, this book also includes references and appendices.

2. INDIA IN INFORMATION AGE

Any sufficiently advanced technology is indistinguishable from magic. ~ Arthur C. Clarke.

2.1. Background

India was one of the richest[1] nations in the world until 1800s. Economy started nose-diving after India's colonisation thanks to pro-Britain trade policies and lack of economic planning. Exploitation of capital and raw materials by European and native rulers further hurt the economy. For half a century before independence, the Indian economy was almost stagnant. Massive engagement in two world wars[2] plummeted Indian economy to an all time low[3]. Later the world's largest population transfer[4] completely shattered Indian economy. Economic growth picked up within a few years after independence and averaged to 3.5 percent from 1950 to 1980 (Das 2002). Despite of the upheavals in the economy, India's love and respect for education, knowledge, research and innovation never dwindled.

Since independence, India has been showing consistent success in the areas of advanced technologies. Besides education, literature, movie-making[5] and beauty pageants, Indians have excelled in the areas of science and technology in India and abroad. Nuclear power, space research, missile launch technology, oceanography, biotechnology etc., are some examples of India's exemplary success in the area of science and technology (see Appendix E for more information).

---

[1] It was the world's largest economy with 32.9 per cent share of world GDP in the 1st Century AD to 24.5 per cent in 1500 AD (Das 2006).
[2] Over 280,000 Indian soldiers participated in First World War. With over 2.5 million men, the Indian Army became the largest all-volunteer force in history during World War II. Indian soldiers won 30 Victoria Crosses and many other decorations for Second World War.
[3] Between 1900 and 1950, economic growth averaged 0.8 percent a year.
[4] Population transfer was a part of the partition of India.
[5] Indian film industry is the world's largest in terms of number of films made and the number of cinema halls.

2.2. Early Computerization in India

India is among the pioneers to utilise the capability of computers in education, Research and Development (R&D), planning and public welfare. First computer arrived in India in 1950. Table 1 shows the chronology of some important events in the history of computers in India.

Table 1: Chronology of Computers in India

Year	Event
1950	First Analog Computer at The Indian Statistical Institute (ISI), Kolkata
1961	First commercial computer installed by ESSO Standard Eastern Inc., Mumbai
1962-1964	14 computers installed in various R &D organizations
1963	IBM 1620 at Indian Institute of Technology(IIT), Kanpur
1965	Tata Institute of Fundamental Research, Mumbai gets a CDC 3600
1965-1966	30 commercial installations
1966	IBM 7044 at IIT, Kanpur
1967	10 Honeywell Computers at Department of Statistics, Cabinet Secretariat
1968	IBM 1401 at IIT, Kanpur
1969	IBM computer at Planning Commission under a grant of Ford Foundation
1978	CMC takes over former IBM maintenance operations
1986	country's first nationwide SNA network, INDONET
1987	First nationwide VSAT network NICNET
1988	NCST established first email link with the USA

Source: National Informatics Centre (NIC) Sangrur[6] and others.

2.3. History of IT in India

As seen in previous section, India acquired first computer in 1950. The Computer Society of India was established in 1965. After the Indo-China war, the government of India set up the Electronics Committee[7] headed by the renowned nuclear scientist Dr. Homi J. Bhabha to plan an indigenous informatics sector. Department of Electronics (DOE) was set up in 1970. Later in February 1971, the Electronics Commission was set up. Information Planning and Analysis Group (IPAG) was constituted within the Electronics Commission in October 1971. Effective

---

[6] Sangrur - National Informatics Center (URL: http://sangrur.nic.in/html/nic_sangrur.html)
[7] In 1966, the committee suggested the establishment of a National Computer Centre and five regional centers with a goal of computer self-sufficiency within 10 years.

policy formulation and implementation for the electronics and computer industry was the objectives of the IPAG. The Electronics Corporation of India Ltd (ECIL) started manufacturing smaller mini computers in India under license from ICL (UK) in 1967. Mainframes and large minis were imported and micro computers were manufactured locally. ECIL had a computer installation market share of 40-50% from early to mid 1970s. By 1988, there were 250 computer manufacturers in India (Singhal and Rogers 1989). In 1975, Burroughs of USA entered into a joint venture with Tata Consultancy Services to manufacture mainframe computers and export software.

Things were smooth until 1977 when something strange happened that later changed the Indian IT scene forever. Then Janata Party government asked foreign companies to align with the Foreign Exchange Regulations Act (FERA) by diluting their equity to 40% in their Indian operations. IBM refused to do so and quit its India operations. IBM customers in India were left without any support. As a consequence the state-owned Computer Maintenance Corporation (CMC) took over the responsibility of the maintenance of all IBM systems in the country. Another consequence of IBM's departure was that UNIX and COBOL gained popularity which would later place India as the world rescuer from the Y2K problem. The market saw a number of IBM competitors ready to respect and accept FERA and other Indian regulations. Indian private sector emerged and companies such as HCL, DCM etc., left ECIL behind. Athreye (2005) considers IBM's departure as the single most important event during this period as it created an import substituting opportunity for domestic manufacturers of computers. The exit of IBM also provided an opportunity for foreign companies such as Burroughs and ICL. Both types of companies depended on Indian programmers to write software conversion programs that could be used for migration from IBM to the new computer systems (Athreye 2005).

Around same time in Bangalore, Bharat Electronics Ltd (BEL) was manufacturing electronic equipment including indigenous minicomputers and operating systems for Indian defense establishments. Computer Science departments were newly opened in engineering colleges. First undergraduate courses in computer science and computer engineering at an IIT were started at Kanpur in 1978. The National Institute of Information Technology (NIIT) was formed in India as a pioneer of computer education in 1981. Slowly, Indian firms started realizing the low cost engineering in India as their global advantage.

Rajiv Gandhi, then Prime Minister of India, announced a new computer policy in 1984 that promoted the use of latest technology to manufacture computers in India at internationally comparable prices. It encouraged use of computers in government departments for economic and social development, and encouraged joint ventures with foreign partners. By 1990 the three top firms in India were software firms (Mulhearn 2000).

In 1987, public sector CMC successfully implemented a nation wide reservation system for the Indian Railways[8]. They became international when they implemented a project in Syria, earned a contract with the London subway system, and a few contracts in other countries. While India was progressing in IT sector, it was making strides in Satellite technology too. Progress in these two sectors helped each other. In 1988, the National Informatics Centre set up a satellite-based communications network called NICNET connecting all major district headquarters. Y2K problem presented a unique opportunity before India. It made India's presence visible to the outside world for the first time. In words of Michael Mandelbaum[9], "Y2K should be called Indian Inter-dependence Day," because it was India's ability to collaborate with Western companies" (Friedman 2005, p79).

2.4. Major IT Players in India

India's IT success story was conceived by the commitment of the government, brought into reality by the dedication of the public sector, turned into a success by the involvement of the private sector and sustained by the quality, affordability and motivation of the workforce. Table 2 lists some important Indian companies dealing in outsourcing.

As of June 2006, more than 1000 IT companies in India were members of National Association of Software and Services Companies (NASSCOM). The combined revenue of

---

[8] Transporting over 5 billion passengers and over 350 million tonnes of freight annually on railroads covering a total length of 63,140 km (39,200 miles) Indian Railways is one of the largest and busiest rail networks in the world. It is also the largest employer on the planet.
[9] Mandelbaum is a foreign policy expert at Johns Hopkins.

NASSCOM member companies constitutes almost 95 percent of the revenue of the IT software and services industry in India.

Table 2: Major Indian Outsourcing Players

Company	Specialty	Low-Cost Locations	Offshore Revenue Range
Infosys Technologies	Software Development, Network Support, Banking, Mortgage Processing	India, Czech Republic, China, USA, Australia	$1-5 billion
Tata Consultancy Services	Software Development, R&D/Engineering, F&A, Telecom, Transportation, Hospitality Operations	India, Hungary, Brazil, Uruguay, Chile, China	$1-5 billion
Wipro	Software Development, R&D/Engineering, Demand Management, Mortgage Processing, Transportation Operations, Healthcare Operations, Banking, Mortgage Processing	India, Canada	$1 -5 billion
Patni Computer Systems	Software Development, Network Support, R&D/Engineering	India	$500 -999 million
HCL Technologies	Software Development, Network Support, R&D/Engineering, Financial Services	India	$500-999 million
Satyam	Software Development, Network Support, R&D/Engineering	India, China, Hungary, Brazil, Australia	$500 -999 million
ExlService Holdings, Inc.	Insurance, Transportation Operations	India	Below $100 million
ICICI OneSource	Call centers	India	Below $100 million
Mphasis Corp.	Financial Services	India, China, Australia	Below $100 million
WNS Global Services	Transportation Operations, Healthcare Operations, Banking, Mortgage Processing	India, Sri Lanka	Below $100 million
24/7 Customer	Customer Service	India, Philippines	Below $100 million

Source: Gartner Inc., Company Reports, Business Week (2006).

2.5. Clusters or regions

The growth of IT sector in India is not homogeneous. It is mainly due to the unequal distribution of infrastructure and other background strengths. Indian IT industry is largely concentrated in South India with Bangalore being the Pioneer whereas Hyderabad and Chennai being early adapters and in close competition with Bangalore. The northern centres are restricted to the National Capital Region comprising of Noida, Gurgaon and Delhi. Pune and Kolkata are two other centres worth mentioning. Figure 1 presents an overview of these clusters and firms situated in them.

Table 3: Key Companies in Major Centers

City/Cluster	Key companies (not exhaustive)
Navi Mumbai / Mumbai / Thane	ABN Amro, Morgan Stanley, Citigroup, Accenture, Tata Consultancy Services, World Network Services
New Delhi / Gurgaon / Noida	Genpact, Sapient, HCL Technologies, American Express, McKinsey research center, E-Funds Corporation
Bangalore	JP Morgan, Goldman Sachs, Siemens, Infosys, Wipro, Tata Consultancy Services, Cognizant Technology Services, Genpact
Chennai	Citigroup, Standart Chartered, World Bank, Ford, Hewlett Packard, AIG, Infosys, Tata Consultancy Services, Cognizant Technology Services
Hyderabad/Secunderabad	HSBC, Microsoft, Franklin Templeton, Infosys, Wipro, Tata Consultancy Services, Cognizant Technology Services, Genpact
Pune	
Kolkata	HSBC, Genpact, IBM, Infosys, Tata Consultancy Services, Cognizant Technology Services

Source: IBEF- KPMG (2006).

Initially the software industry was mainly concentrated in Mumbai (Heeks 1996). The traditional industrial centres gradually trailed behind Bangalore. This fact reflects a linear relationship of the growth of IT with the number of institutions of specialised education and research. Figure 8 illustrates that the growth and distribution of intake in engineering degrees which provided for the required trained human capital is higher in south India. The concentration of the IT industry in Bangalore, Chennai and Hyderabad is due to the availability of higher educational setup. One issue with cluster based development is the rising cost. This is not a limiting factor considering the size of India and its education system. Industry is moving to second tier cities in India. The fact that companies like Meinhardt International from Singapore decided to move its focus from China to India, shows that overall cost in India is still lower despite of comparatively higher wages. Indian IT industry is slowly unshackling from the clusters. The gap between original and the second-tier cities is weaning off. The region of cluster is spreading fast to cover cities such as Ahmedabad, Jaipur, Coimbatore, Kochi, Trivandrum, Chandigarh, Mysore, Mangalore, Madurai and Bhubhaneswar. In fact it is unfair to call Bangalore, Delhi, Mumbai, Chennai and Hyderabad as clusters anymore. These five cities are the IT hubs of India and the clusters have already spread around all STPI zones.

3.   MEASURING THE SUCCESS

India has become an emerging economic power to the betterment of its people.
~ George W. Bush[10], U.S President (July 18, 2005).

Indian scientists, educators, doctors, engineers are known for their expertise, dedication and work culture. Its skilled workforce makes it an obvious choice for international companies seeking to outsource work. Indian IT sector is growing so well that India is fast becoming a synonym of IT. In some areas, such as BPO, India is the undisputed leader. Our survey explored that IT professionals started noticing India's success in IT during late 1980s. This chapter is an attempt to make sure that this success is not hype.

3.1. Reality or Hype

India had achieved similar success in other areas of advanced technology and research. But the success in IT touched people's lives in developed countries to a large extent. It gave a boost to the economy in countries like USA, Singapore, and Australia. At the same time, it was depicted as a threat to local economies by some politicians in USA and Germany. No wonder one German politician cried "Kinder, nicht Inder"[11] (children, not Indians) when Germany invited 20,000 Indian engineers on IT-related work visas. Several groups have been formed in the USA to oppose or completely eliminate H1B visas[12] and outsourcing. Out of an estimated 900,000 H1-B employees in the US, around 40 percent are from India, according to American Immigration Lawyers Association.

---

[10] Public Interest Service (URL: http://releases.usnewswire.com/GetRelease.asp?id=50449)
[11] The Occidental Quarterly (URL: http://theoccidentalquarterly.com/vol3no4/dt-euroright.html)
[12] The H-1B program is for a temporary visa that allows American companies and universities to employ foreign scientists, engineers, programmers, and other professionals in the United States.

3.2. Competitiveness

It's not that India is successful; certain regions have been particularly successful, and those regions are driving the whole country...India has a tremendous tendency for overstatement. ~ Michael E. Porter[13].

The Global Competitiveness Index (GCI) is a part of the Global Competitiveness Report[14] (GCR) which is prepared by the World Economic Forum. Initiated in 2001, the GCR ranks nations by their microeconomic competitiveness, identifies competitive strengths and weaknesses in terms of business environment and company operations and strategies, and assesses the sustainability of current levels of prosperity as measured by per capita GDP adjusted for purchasing power. The GCI includes nine parameters:

- infrastructure
- institutions
- macro-economy
- health and primary education
- higher education and training
- market efficiency
- technological readiness
- business sophistication
- innovation.

Except for health and primary education, India has scored well on above GCI parameters especially on innovation, institutions, business sophistication and higher education and training. As per the GCR for 2006-07, India stands 43 in the ascending order among 121 countries while China was ranked 54 and USA ranked six.

Michael E. Porter of Harvard Business School has devised another system similar to the GCI in 2000 which is now called Business Competitive Index (BCI). Table 3 shows that India

---

[13] Harvard Business School's Michael E. Porter in an interview with Manjari Raman published on December 29, 2004. URL: http://inhome.rediff.com/money/2004/dec/29inter.htm
[14] World Economic Forum (URL: http://www.weforum.org/gcr)

moved up to 27th place in BCI from 31 a year ago. China trailed farther behind at 64 from 54 in 2004[15].

Table 3: BCI Ranks of India, China and USA

Country	2006	2005	2004
India	27	31	31
China	64	54	48
USA	1	1	1

According to Kearney Offshore Location Attractiveness Study of 2005, the Indian IT industry ranks highest (see Figure 2) in terms of attractiveness for investment among all competing countries.

China maintains second place while USA is at 11th position. India remains the best offshore location by a wide margin, although wage inflation and the emergence of lower-cost countries decreased its overall lead (Kearney 2005).

---

[15]India's upwardly move in BCI becomes more significant due to the fact that in December 2004, Porter dismissed India's progress as an overstatement.

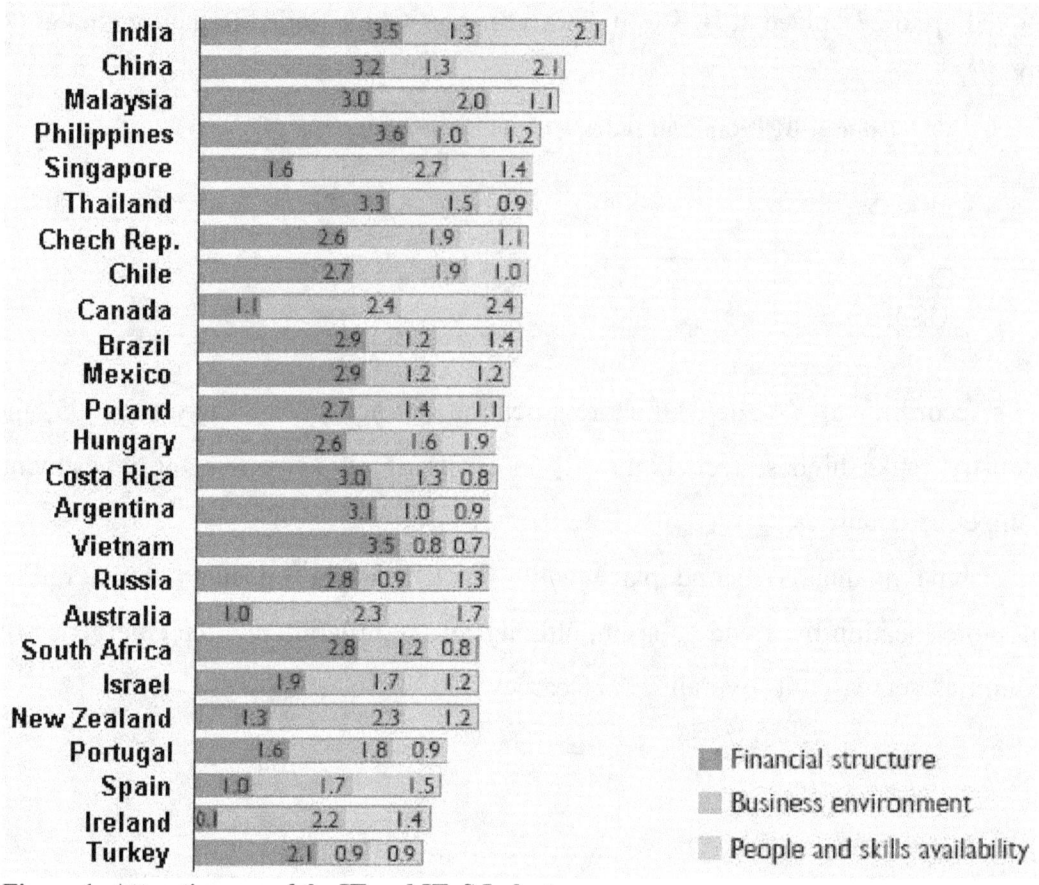

Figure 1: Attractiveness of the IT and ITeS Industry

Source: AT Kearney Offshore Location Attractiveness Study 2005

3.3. Some Indicators

Eighty out of the world's 117 SEI CMM Level 5 companies[16] are from India. Over 100 of the Fortune500 companies have set up R&D centres in India. India recently launched Param Padma, its fourth generation super computer with a peak computing power of a teraflop, conceived and manufactured indigenously by the Centre for the Development of Advanced Computing (C-DAC). India produces 3 million graduates, 700,000 post-graduates and 1,500

---

[16]SEI CMM Level 5 is a capability maturity model with five phases, developed by the Software Engineering Institute (SEI) of the Carnegie Mellon University, Pittsburgh.

PhDs every year. In addition to these facts, a survey conducted by NASSCOM highlights some clear indicators of the success of IT in India (NASSCOM 2006b):

- Indian net earning from software export for the financial year 2004-05 is $17.5 billion.

- The Indian IT-ITES industry has recorded 33 per cent growth in exports, clocking revenues of US$ 23.6 billion in FY 2005-06.

- Overall Indian IT-ITES industry (including domestic market) grew by 31 per cent registering revenues of US$ 29.6 billion in FY 2005-06.

- Of the total IT-ITES exports in FY 2005-06, IT software and services grew by 33 per cent, registering revenues of US$ 13.3 billion.

- The ITES-BPO segment clocked revenues of US$ 6.2 billion, recording a growth of 37 per cent.

- Engineering services and product exports grew from US$ 3.14 billion in FY 04-05 to US$ 4 billion in FY 05-06.

- Domestic market clocked revenues of US$ 6 billion in FY 04-05 from US$ 4.8 billion in FY 05-06.

3.4. Mergers and Acquisitions (M&A)

Indian IT companies are using M&A to increase presence in USA and Europe. India has become the second largest investor in Britain next to the USA. Almost half of these acquisitions were in IT. According to a Yahoo news report[17], Indian companies spent 228 million pounds[18] buying British businesses in 2005. Some examples of the 2006 acquisitions and joint ventures undertook abroad by Indian IT industry in last quarter of 2006 are listed below[19]:

---

[17] Source: http://in.news.yahoo.com/061206/43/6a1vf.html
[18] The value of the average Indian takeover in Britain rose to 28.5 million pounds compared with 6 million pounds in 2004.
[19] BusinessLine (URL: http://www.thehindubusinessline.com/cgi-bin/bl.pl?subclass=348)

- Indian Telecom software firm Subex Systems $140 million deal to acquire UK-based Azure Solutions is the largest foreign acquisition by an Indian IT company.

- 3i Infotech paid $12 million to acquire 51 per cent stake in Professional Access of USA.

- Mantas Inc. of USA was acquired by i-flex Solutions Ltd in an all-cash transaction of $122.6 million.

- TransWorks, an Aditya Birla Group acquired a Canada-based BPO company Minacs Worldwide Inc. for $125 million.

- Tata Consultancy Services (TCS) would hold 64 per cent stake in its Chinese joint venture partnered with National Development Reforms Commission (NDRC) and Microsoft.

3.5. IT Research and Development (R&D)

India has now become a research and development (R&D) hub for software. The Indian Institute of Technology, Mumbai has been sanctioned with a total outlay of US$ 22 million over a period of five years. Google set up an R&D centre in India in 2004. Leading web portal Yahoo carries out R&D work in Bangalore. Intel is already established in India while Intersil Corporation[20] is setting up a design centre in Bangalore. IBM has set up a research lab in Delhi. Nokia plans to set up R&D hub in India[21]. The Council of Scientific & Industrial Research (CSIR) obtained 542 US patents between 2002 and 2005. Nature nicknamed CSIR as India's patent factory[22] because its US patents exceeded the total number of patents granted to its counterparts in France, Japan and Germany combined. There were 23,000 patent applications filed in 2005-06, up from 17,466 in 2004-06. Table 4 shows the number of patents filed by some Indian and multi national companies (MNCs) (Chakravorty 2006).

Table 4: Patents filed by MNCs and Indian Firms (on facing page)

---

[20] USA based chipmaker.
[21] Source: India Brand Equity Foundation and various news channels.
[22] Telugu Portal (http://www.teluguportal.net/modules/news/article.php?storyid=12282)

Company	Filed in 2004-05	Granted in 2004-05	Filed in 2005-06	Granted in 2005-06
MNCs				
Adobe Systems	10	-	32	-
Cadence	1	5	-	-
Flextronics	2	1	4	1
Freescale	10	-	16	4
Microsoft	40	-	70	-
ST Micro	62	32	37	14
Symantec	47	43	57	16
Texas Instruments	35	10	-	-
Indian				
i-flex	1	-	1	-
Infosys	-	-	20	-
Mindtree	1	-	2	-
Ramco	16	-	16	-
Sasken	5	-	5	5
Subex	-	-	2	-
TCS	16	5	13	4

Source: Chakravorty (2006).

3.6. Business Process Outsourcing (BPO)

BPO gave a big boost to Indian IT industry in last few years. Recent acquisitions of the Indian BPO companies by global giants like Accenture and IBM show the strength and demand for the Indian BPO market. The BPO Sector has been growing at 50% annually. Its turnover in 2004-05 reached US$ 5.8 billion from US$ 565 million in 1999-2000. It is projected to increase to US$ 12.3 billion by 2006 and create employment opportunities for a million people from its current level of 200,000. Some highlights of the Indian ITeS-BPO industry[23] are shown in Table 5. Indian BPO has helped the companies deliver products faster at lower costs. These companies have developed global competence.

---

[23] BPO Knowledgebase (URL: http://www.bpoindia.org/knowledgeBase/)

Table 5: Indian BPO Snapshots

ITeS-BPO	2002-03	2003-04	2004-05	2005-06
Exports ($ bn)	2.5	3.6	5.2	7.3
Domestic ($ bn)	0.2	0.3	0.3	0.8
Total Employment (,000)	171	245	348	470

Source: Rediff (2005).   (Figures in US $ billions)

3.7. IT Revenue

IT industry is one of the fastest growing industries in India. It also contributes over 25% of total service sector export from India. It is getting more sophisticated with time (see Figures 3 and 4). Today, Indian IT industry is known for innovation, quality and dependability besides overall savings in terms of cost and time.

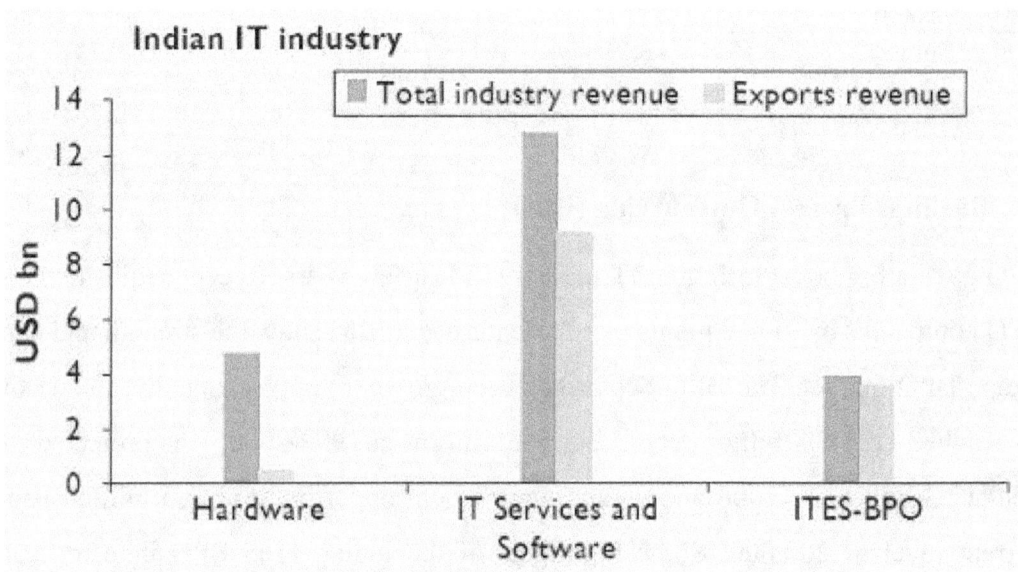

Figure 2: Revenue Earned by Indian IT Industry

Source: IBEF-KPMG (2006)

28

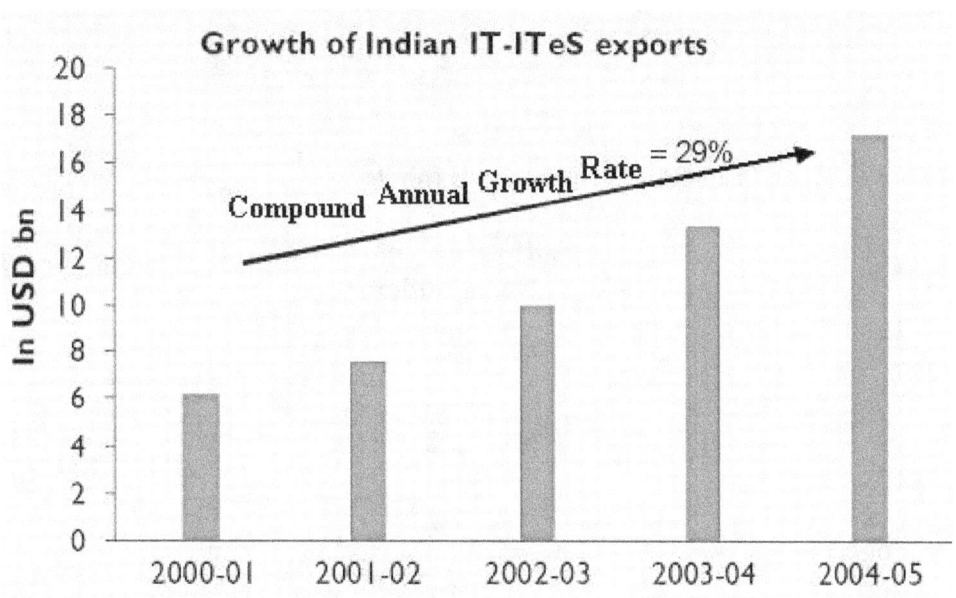

Figure 3: Exports Performance of IT-ITeS sector

Source: IBEF-KPMG (2006)

Even assuming a conservative growth rate of 20 percent[24], Indian IT-ITeS exports could reach US$ 42 billion by 2010. It is obvious from the official figures that India's software and service export industry is booming. Revenue from the export of software and from services sold to companies from outside India reached $17.2 billion during fiscal 2004-2005, according to NASSCOM. The average annual growth rate for ten years from 1994-95 to 2004-05 is 38%. Table 6 shows that the growth in Indian software export is consistently in double digits.

---

[24] India Brand Equity Foundation – Davos 2006 (URL: http://ibef.org/download/IT_sectoral.pdf)

Table 6: Growth in Indian Software Exports

Year	Software Exports (US $ in millions)	Export Growth (%)
1980	4.0	-
1981	6.8	70
1982	13.5	99
1983	18.2	35
1984	25.3	39
1985	27.7	9.5
1986	38.9	40
1987	54.1	38
1988-89 (Apr-Mar)	69.7	29
1989-90	105.4	51
1990-91	131.2	24
1991-92	173.9	33
1992-93	219.8	26
1993-94	314.0	43
1994-95	480.9	53
1995-96	668.0	39
1996-97	997.0	49
1997-98	1650	65
1998-99	2180	32
1999-2000	3600	65
2000-01	5300	47
2001-02	6200	17
2002-03	7550	22
2003-04	12800	41
2004-05	17200	34.5
2005-06	21957	21.7

Source: Heeks (1996), Dataquest (1998), NASSCOM (2006).

3.8. IT Workforce

It is an understatement to say that India plays a critical role in offshore software development; indeed, India pioneered the concept. India is respected world wide as a growing technological power, and produces some of the best educated and most capable software engineers in the world today. ~Dr. Clark M. Sykes[25], (Vice President, Information Technology, Merchants Insurance Companies)

Sixty percent of India's population is between the ages 15-59, and more than half is under 25. India will provide a long-term supply of knowledge professionals. In contrast, countries like US, Japan and China have a more aged population with dependency ratios likely to increase over the same period (NASSCOM 2006a).

The number of knowledge professionals in India is growing in absolute numbers as well as in percentage of the total work force. Figure 5 taken from Niles (1999) confirms that the information technology employees have superseded the workers in agriculture, manufacturing or service sectors each.

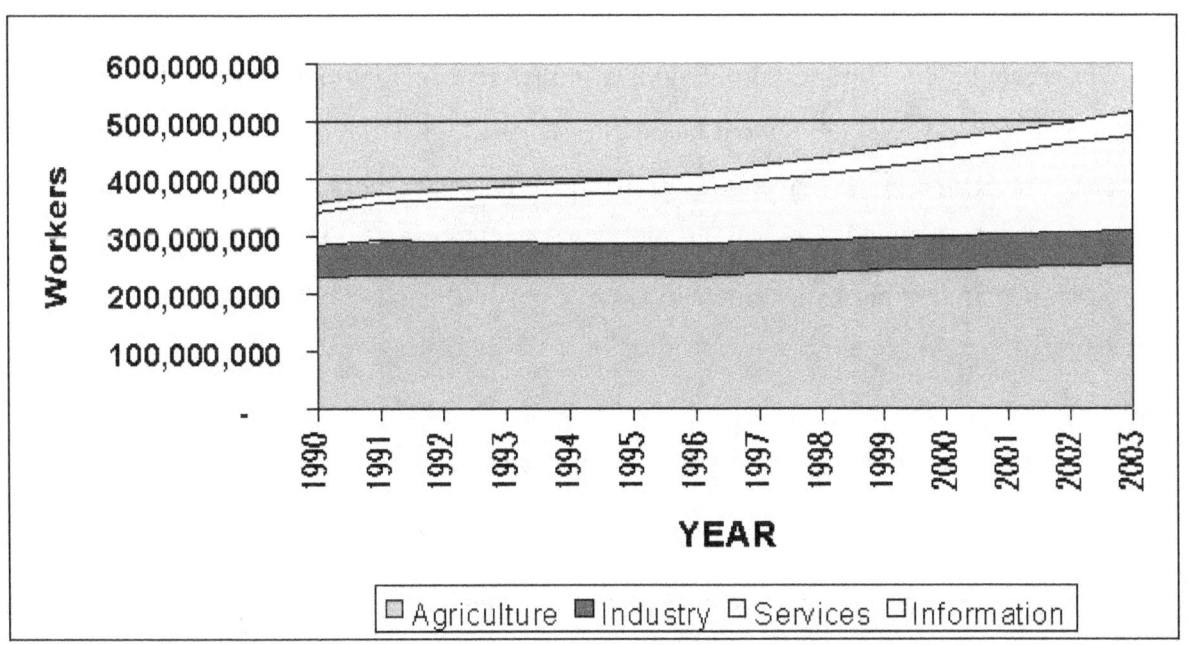

Figure 4: Estimated Composition of the Workforce in India

---

[25] MindTree Consulting (URL: http://www.mindtree.com/clt/interview-vp-clark-m-sykes.htm)

As shown in Figure 6, the total number of IT and ITES professionals employed in India has grown from 284,000 in 1999-2000 to over 1 million in 2004-05, growing by over 200,000 in the last year alone (NASSCOM 2005a).

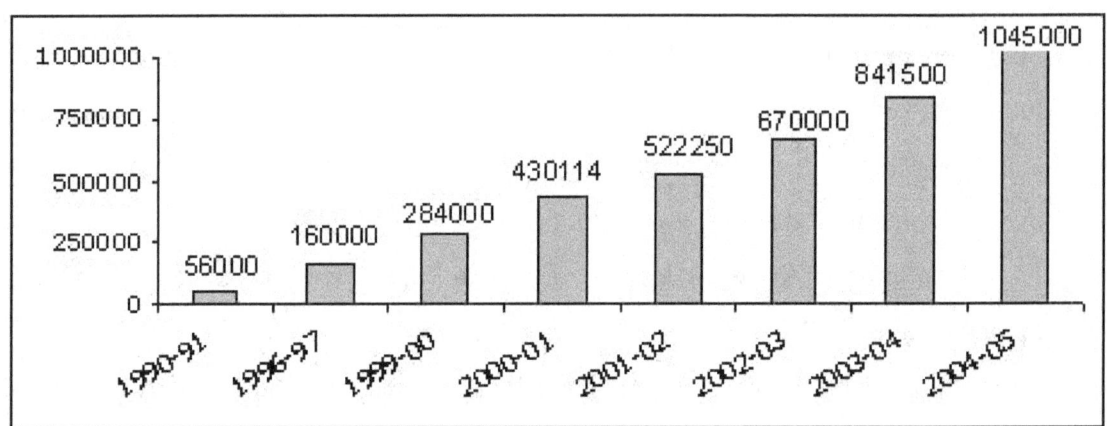

Figure 5: Growth of Manpower Employed in Indian Software Industry

(Source: NASSCOM 2006a)

A break-up of the 1 million professionals in different sectors indicate that the number of employees in the ITES-BPO segment has witnessed the highest levels of growth over the last few years – attributed to the tremendous growth in demand for these services. ITES companies recruited around 100,000 professionals in 2004-05. Companies in the IT software exports sector recruited 75,000 professionals in 2004-05, compared to 65,000 professionals recruited in 2003-04 (NASSCOM 2006a).

Table 7: Sector wise Manpower Employed in Indian Software Industry

Sector	2001-02	2002-03	2003-04	2004-05
Software Exports sector	170,000	205,000	270,000	345,000
Software-domestic sector	22,000	25,000	28,000	30,000
Software- in house captive staff	224,250	260,000	290,000	322,000
ITES-BPO	106,000	180,000	253,500	348,000
Total	**522,250**	**670,000**	**841,500**	**1,045,000**

Source: NASSCOM's Strategic Review of 2003, 2004, 2005.

3.9. Foreign Direct Investment (FDI)

India suggests that FDI is not the only path to prosperity[26]. India's home-grown entrepreneurs may give it a long-term advantage over a China hamstrung by inefficient banks and capital markets. ~ Dr Yasheng Huang[27],

FDI inflows into India increased 47 percent to $1.7 billion in April-June quarter of 2006, compared to $1.1 billion in the same period in 2005. During 2005-2006, the FDI inflow was $8.2 billion (Srivastava 2006). The low FDI numbers highlight a distinct feature of the Indian economy. Independence from FDI displays the inner strength of the Indian enterprise. Indian IT industry is no exception. India's brand of well-known IT giants like Infosys Technologies, TCS and Wipro are born and bred locally without any support through FDI. This conclusion is also supported by Athreye (2005) while stating that the Indian software industry stands out in terms of the volume of employment created and the indigenous nature of its growth.

3.10. Gross Domestic Product (GDP)

Table 8 shows that the GDP in India has increased consistently and the share of IT and ITeS industry is on the rise. By 2010, IT will account for 7% of India's GDP.

---

[26] In a lecture at SJM School of Management in IIT Bombay on October 25, 2004.
[27] Dr Yasheng Huang is a noted economist. He is currently a Professor at the MIT Sloan School of Management.

Table 8: IT as part of India's GDP

Year	GDP (Rs. in billion)	IT-ITeS Sector (Rs. in billion)	IT-ITeS Sector (% of GDP)
1991-1992	6168	-	-
1994-1995	9170	63	0.7
1995-1996	10986	99	0.9
1996-1997	12435	137	1.1
1997-1998	13900	186.4	1.2
1998-1999	16160	253.1	1.5
1999-2000	17923	361.8	1.9
2000-2001	18704	565.9	2.7
2001-2002	19781	657.9	2.9
2002-2003	20526	779.6	3.2
2003-2004	22260	978.3	3,5
2004-2005	23937	1275.8	4.1

Source: NASSCOM and Various News Channels

3.11. Summary

It is clear from the data and facts that India's success in IT is real. India is also consolidating the gains further. Also, contrary to general belief, India's success is not limited to IT. India has been an achiever in other advanced areas too such as space research and nuclear science etc. India's advancement in other high tech sectors did not attract media attention because it did not affect life of a common citizen in developed countries the way IT did.

4. CHALLENGES

No doubt, India has fared better than expected in IT and other high tech areas. It still has its own share of challenges which need to be addressed to sustain the progress. Following sections highlight major roadblocks and analyze their effect on development in India especially in IT sector.

4.1. Poverty and Financial Disparity

Wherever I go when I am in Britain, I find India is known for two things - poverty and population. ~ Mark Tully[28], BBC correspondent in India.

India is a land of contrasts. Despite of various poverty eradication initiatives, the estimated percentage of poverty for 2006 is 22, an improvement[29] from 26 in 1999-2000. Poverty is a major drawback for India's progress. It needs to be addressed more effectively. IT has generated millions of jobs for the educated and highly skilled in last few decades. These professionals are creating demand for housing, banking, insurance, and other consumer sections that help the economy grow. IT sector is creating jobs for the under-privileged also for positions of security staff, caterers, transporters, construction workers etc. IT is being used directly in many poverty alleviation projects sponsored by the government, industry and non-government organisations (NGOs). India's Information and Communication Technology sector provides direct employment to approximately 800,000 rural poor people. This number is expected to rise to 2.2 million by the year 2008.

4.2. Population

Uncontrolled growth of population in India is considered a social, economic, and environmental problem. If the rate of population growth is not checked drastically, India may

---

[28]BBC News
(URL: http://news.bbc.co.uk/2/hi/programmes/from_our_own_correspondent/3602862.stm)
[29]The poverty percentage was 36% in 1993-94 and 54 in 1974-75. The reduction from 54% to 22% in 30 years shows the willpower and capability of India.

overtake China by 2050 according to Washington-based Population Reference Bureau. A growing population can make the already limited resources stretched beyond safe limits.

Population has been traditionally considered as a burden to the economy. But, we should not forget that it is India's population that provides us the most valuable resource. Human resources have emerged as the main contributing factor to India's success in IT and other advanced industries. Currently, all major economies are concerned about aging population and negative growth. After Europe and Japan it is China's turn to worry about aging population[30]. India is projected to maintain the lead for largest young population till 2025.

Though India has an excellent ratio of younger-older population, lower fertility rate will certainly help poor population of India. Targeted efforts are needed to reduce poverty and provide basic amenities including sanitation, drinking water, health care and education to the poor. Poor people in India consider their children as insurance in their old age. This feeling can be removed only by providing better living conditions which should be the top priority of the government and all capable citizens.

4.3. Illiteracy

We have one of the world's largest reservoirs of technical personnel, but also the world's largest number of illiterates. ~ K.R. Narayanan, Former President of India.

India's IT success is an exception of the common belief that illiteracy and development are two opposite poles. There is another side of the coin specific to India, often ignored by the analysts. The majority of the artisans, farmers and blue-collar workers of India have no or minimal formal schooling. So was the Nobel Laureate Rabindranath Tagore who has the unparalleled honour of being the author of the national anthems for two countries, India and Bangladesh. Though most of the illiterates of India are able to do arithmetical operation routinely and have expertise of their trade, India has to travel a lot on path of providing education to all citizens.

---

[30]Forcible implementation of one-child policy for last 25-years has started showing its negative effect. The number of elderly Chinese people is expected to top 200 million by 2015 and 280 million by 2025. Around 30 percent of the population would be classified as elderly by 2050, according to the Communist Party newspaper People's Daily.

A recent World Bank survey (Figure 7) found that 25% of government primary school teachers in India are absent from work while only half of the teachers were actually teaching while at work (Kremer et al. 2005).

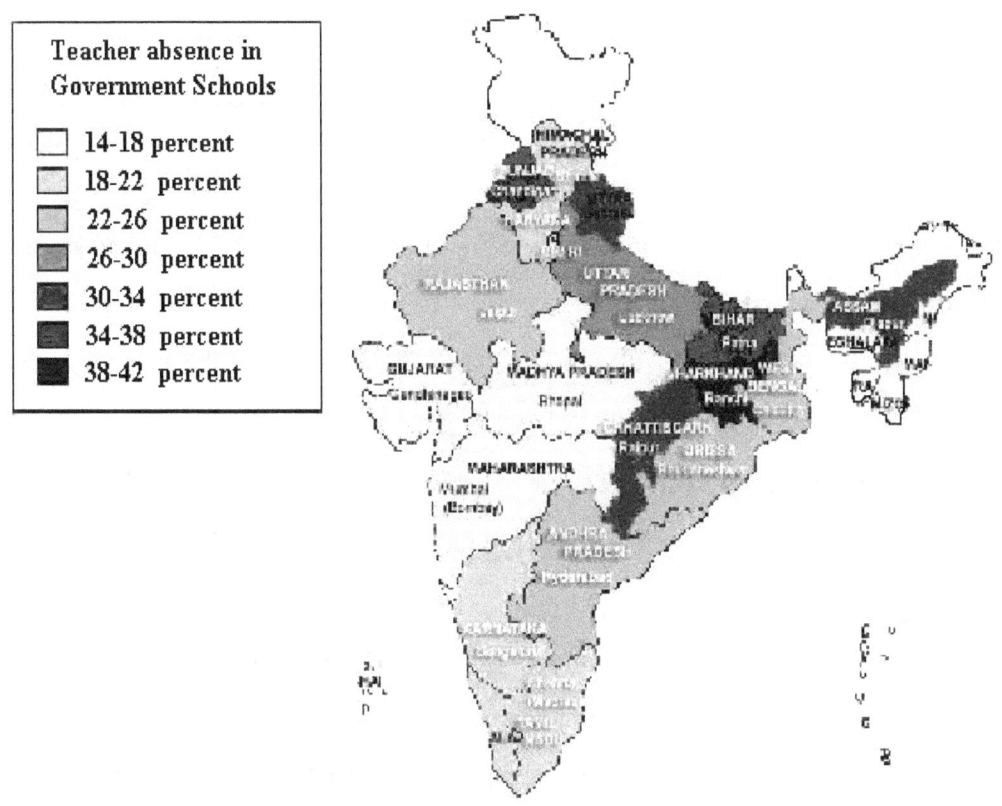

Figure 6: Teacher Absenteeism in Indian Public Schools

A large part of population has no means to get education and a larger part is not able to get it because the teachers and administrators in the large network of public schools have failed miserably in executing their duties. Before boasting about the higher education revolution, India needs to do a lot in providing basic education to hitherto deprived children. Also, India needs to improve the quality of public schools and the teachers.

4.4. Digital Divide

In a developed country, Digital Divide is a matter of concern for the companies considering the other side of the divide as lost customers. In a country like India where a large population lives below poverty line, the phrase "digital divide" is almost meaningless. Even if the village Panchayat[31] has a computer, it is of no use to a homeless without food, water or medicine. To stay ahead of the curve, India has to manage more basic issues such as drinking water, health, education and poverty before worrying about the digital divide.

On the other hand, the major market for an average IT company in India is still overseas - another reason the digital divide is not a major concern today. It is a problem of future and the Government has to work hand-in-hand with the industry and NGOs. These issues can be tackled with help of proper training, micro-credit and a vision as displayed in the past by Mr. Sam Pitroda in making the telephone accessible to the poorest population in the remotest areas. An Indian innovation such as Simputer[32] is one of the practical steps taken in right direction. Stress on open source is another one to help spread of IT across the less-privileged sections.

4.5. Inadequate Investment in R&D

India's large-scale industry avoided investment in R&D and innovations in the past. Government initiatives and direct funding of R&D institutions may help achieving the objectives over the next decade. But the journey will not be easy (Parthasarathi 2003).

The fact is that research is gaining momentum in India and India is becoming a R&D hub of the world. Over the past few years, over 100 of the Fortune 500 MNCs have set up R&D centers in India with total investment of over US$ one billion. Leading companies like GE, Bell Labs, Cummins, DuPont, Daimler Chrysler, Eli Lilly, General Motors, Hewlett Packard, Intel, Honeywell, Qualcomm and Whirlpool have set up R&D centers in India. Domestic research institutions too have realized the importance of getting their inventions patented in USA. The patent portfolio of 38 publicly funded Indian laboratories has increased from fewer than 30 U.S. patents in 1995 to more than 720 in July 2006[33]. Though the raw patent numbers are quite small, it is a good beginning.

---

[31]The Panchayat is an elected body in an Indian village. It is the smallest building block of the Indian democratic system that provides power to the grass root level.
[32] Simputer is a simple tablet-pc like device (URL: http://www.simputer.org/)
[33] MIT Technology Review
(URL: http://www.technologyreview.com/read_article.aspx?id=17339&ch=biztech)

4.6. Lack of Infrastructure

India has a well established network of rail roads, hospitals, schools, banks, insurance and other institutions. New Delhi's new $2 billion subway system called Metro is impressive. It is being studied for implementation in other Indian cities. Most of Indian cities have already started following Delhi's lead of using compressed natural gas (CNG) for public transportation system. India adds 7.5 kilometres (4.5 miles) to its existing highway network every day. Around 250,000 people are currently employed in an ambitious nationwide project called Golden Quadrangle to upgrade 45,000 kilometres of national highways at a cost of $40 billion.

In 2006, India's Power Finance Corporation signed an agreement with the National Rural Electric Cooperative Association of USA and the World Bank to set up a public-private partnership for rural electricity distribution and advisory services. This alliance is an important step toward India's goal of achieving universal electrification by 2012[34]. Similarly, a private sector company Posco is included in a $900 million project to build a seaport in Orissa.

Despite of all these efforts, the fact is that the infrastructure has been ignored for pretty long time in the past. India has a serious shortage of power to support the industries. The total infrastructure investment requirements for the next five years have been estimated around US$ 115-130 billion. Improving power system alone would require approximately $45 billion during the next three years. The task of finding such large amounts and thereafter deploying them productively is not easy. Cluster-centered infrastructure is the preferred alternative for software industry in case of absence of infrastructure on a national basis (Carmel 2003). This is exactly what happened in India. The schemes such as STPI and the regional strengths as in Bangalore helped the growth of the Indian IT industry in spite of lack of infrastructure on national level.

4.7. Corruption

The rampant presence of corruption in India's day to day life is frustratingly high. It is common to bribe a police officer to avoid a traffic ticket or bribe an income tax inspector to avoid tax

---

[34]International Finance Corporation
(URL: http://www.ifc.org/ifcext/media.nsf/Content/India_IFC_Promotes_Innovation_Oct06)

payment. Civil contractors bribe the government authorities to use poor quality material in building roads and bridges. This tolerance of general public towards corruption has been a major hindrance to the development of this great nation. IT plays an important role by reducing the corruption in several ways including the following ones:

- Computerisation of the courts speeds up the disposal of pending cases.
- Evidences can be preserved for a longer period of time without tampering.
- Transparency in government rules reduces incidences of bribery due to ignorance of the victim.
- Good training to police, civil servants and administrators and law makers.

4.8. Nepotism and Cheap Politics

According to the World Economic Forum (WEF), India ranks 57 among 121 countries for favouritism in decisions of Government officials[35]. A recent move of Union Minister for Human Resource Development, Arjun Singh, to impose caste-based job reservations on private sector[36] was vehemently opposed by the industry. In spite of the nationwide protests, the government extended the reservations and concessions to certain castes for admissions in elite institutions such as IITs, Indian Institutes of Management and All India Institute of Medical Sciences too[37]. These policies of cheap popularity are dangerous to the nation and result in social tension and mutual distrust among the communities. These steps divide the country on basis of caste and religion and discourage certain sections of society from being efficient, innovative and hardworking as the world class education and a highly paid job is assured for them whatever happens. Even within strong Indian democracy, some politicians act with authoritarianism and thus harm the national interest[38]. It is very important to save the nation

---

[35]With 43rd position, China is placed much better compared to India.

[36]Indian public sector and government jobs already have caste based reservation ranging from 50-80% positions in these sector reserved for certain castes.

[37]The admissions to the IITs were strictly based on performance in the Joint Entrance Exam (JEE).

[38]Sam Pitroda had to leave India when Prime Minister VP Singh insisted on filling certain positions of power by people of his choice with full disregards to the national interest. The history was repeated when N R Narayana Murthy resigned from the chairmanship of the Bangalore International Airport Limited following personal attacks by former prime minister H D Deve Gowda in 2005.

from whims and fancies of the authoritarian leaders to sustain India's growth in IT and other area.

4.9. Economic Patriotism

European resistance over Mittal Steels' bid to take over Arcelor highlighted the issue of economic patriotism. Similar feelings were reflected by the federal outsourcing restrictions in the USA. Like USA and Europe, India too is not untouched with the growing demand of economic protection from incompetent industrialists. Gandhi's slogan of Swadeshi as a part of independence movement was not the only time when economic patriotism was an issue. India witnessed another Swadeshi movement in 1977 when the Janata Party government asked foreign companies to dilute their equity in Indian firms. As a consequence, IBM chose to leave India in 1978 (Heeks 1996, p 56). The most recent wave of economic patriotism became visible with formation of Swadeshi Jagran Manch in 1991 to protect local industries. Indians should realize that protectionism and economic patriotism is good only for the inefficient businesses and is really bad for the nation and its people.

It is mandatory to build strong, powerful, self-respecting corporations and brands to make India a strong, powerful, self-respecting nation (Nandy 1998). India needs equal opportunities, and equal challenges to prove its strengths and not Swadeshi slogans to support incompetence.

4.10. Wars and Pseudo-Wars

Carving Pakistan out of India on grounds that Muslims cannot live with a multitude of other religions resulted in division of a great nation into two perpetual enemies. Besides a brief border-conflict with China[39], India has fought three wars and several border clashes with Pakistan. Also, India is consistently fighting a war against terrorism and insurgency on its porous borders. India's engagement in wars and internal security costs a lot. It also hinders India from effectively providing basic amenities to its citizens. The high cost of security can be understood better by the fact that after 911 the US airline industry has suffered $42 billion in collective losses from 2001 through 2005.

---

[39]Unable to digest India's asylum to Dalai Lama and support for Tibet and Bhutan and Sikkim, Chinese Peoples Liberation Army (PLA) launched a surprise attack on India in 1962.

The inflow of refugees from conflict torn neighboring countries puts a lot of burden on India. It supports a large number of refugees from Afghanistan, Tibet, Nepal, Bhutan, Burma, Bangladesh and Sri Lanka. Though the root cause of the refugee problem lies outside India and India does not have much control over it, India has learned to face these threats effectively. Also in past decades, India has emerged as a role model in the region and more and more people in the region are realizing the priorities and have started raising voice against the sponsors and supporters of the wars and terrorism.

4.11. Summary

The challenges listed in this chapter can be sub-grouped into three categories depending on their threat level from 0 to 2 where 0 being completely harmless and 2 being the strongest. Digital divide is not a major issue for India as the innovative solutions such as Internet kiosks, tele-cottages and cybercafés are making the technology available to the less privileged class at affordable cost. The real issue is to provide the basic amenities like drinking water for the downtrodden before dreaming of a computer or a satellite phone.

Ashraf (2004) stresses on targeting primary education, basic health services, water and sanitation requirements especially in rural and backward areas. India needs to make sincere efforts to eradicate poverty before worrying about issues such as digital divide. Lack of R&D and infrastructure is getting due attention and a reasonable amount of resources are being directed into these areas and the investment is consistently increasing. The challenges are listed in Table 9 according to the threat level.

Table 9: The Challenges and their Threat Level

Challenge	Threat Level
Tolerance For Unethical Behavior	2
Corruption	2
Poverty	2
Cheap Politics	2
Nepotism	2
Economic Patriotism	2
Terrorism/Insurgency/Wars	1
Job Reservations	1
Illiteracy	1
Population	1
Digital Divide	0
Lack of Infrastructure	0
Lack of R&D	0

Incidences of illiteracy should be given more priority and the political leaders should grow above cheap popularity to address this issue in a mature and practical manner. Instead of adding a new caste every year for reservations in jobs and education, they should try to address the root cause of the problem. Poverty, corruption, nepotism, economic patriotism and cheap politics are some serious challenges before India. People's tolerance for unethical behavior is another challenge that deserves top priority.

5. SUCCESS FACTORS

Many theories have been proposed for India's edge over other competing nations in the IT business. Kapur (2002) attributes low-cost as an advantage of Indian IT industry. Nagala (2005) attributes it to fluency in the English language while some suggest supportive government policy infrastructure and high quality offerings as the leading causes of it. Leading global business intelligence and consultancy firms such as Forrester Research and McKinsey & Co. cite quality and cost benefit advantages as the major differentiators for increasing offshore outsourcing by MNCs to India. Global corporations are generating cost savings in the range of 40-60 per cent, depending on the process off-shored. Manpower costs in India are 70-80 per cent less than in the US and UK. This chapter discusses major advantages that have helped India overcome challenges and maintain a steady and sustainable growth.

5.1. Cultural Advantage

Indian culture values learning of art, philosophy, science and mathematics. The Arabic numerals[40], zero, infinity and the decimal system were invented by the Indians. Indians have developed and studied subjects such as mathematics, metallurgy, astronomy etc. India has an age old tradition of intellectual debates[41]. It is the birthplace of intellectual games such as chess. The fact that current Indian president is a nuclear scientist and all past presidents have been scholars and linguists highlights the emphasis, respect and reward Indian society gives to higher education.

Besides scholarly traditions, India has had a well established tradition of entrepreneurship, banking and trade. India was known as the Golden Bird[42] among foreigners. European nations[43] had cut-throat competition with each other to get a share of trade with India.

---

[40]The Arabic and Persian word for numbers is Hindse which literally means "From India". Although Arabic is written from right to left, the numbers are written left to right proving the foreign affiliation.
[41]Shastrarth is the ancient Indian system of intellectual debates based of meticulously defined rules.
[42]Even today the value of gold in Indian households exceeds 10,000 tons, largest in the world.
[43]Columbus accidentally discovered America while searching for a shorter trade route to India.

India also has an unbiased judiciary and a democratic society. In fact there are historical references of the democratic states as old as 600 BC[44]. It has been the original melting pot of cultures with ethnically and linguistically diverse society with a progressive and open outlook.

These great ancient traditions have helped India to excel in areas that require abstract thinking, advanced science and mathematical abilities, thinking out of the box, innovation and learning a new language or skill. Any nation can become the manufacturing factory of the world but it is natural for India to lead in advanced technologies.

5.2. Freedom

As a global power, India has an historic duty to support democracy around the world. ~George W. Bush, US President (March 3, 2006)[45]

Despite of being surrounded by the communist, religious and military dictatorships, and monarchies, India is world's biggest democracy and a bastion of freedom. It has supported freedom movements all over the world. There were regulations on export and import of certain goods but there have been no restriction on free speech. Internet or any other mode of speech is not censored in India. According to the World Economic Forum (WEF), India ranks 25 among 121 countries in freedom of press[46]. China ranks an abysmally low as 99 in the same report. No wonder news and media industry flourished in India. This free Indian attitude reflects in spread of knowledge and information also. It is a key success factor for the IT industry in India. Information is everything in IT. 95% of people must have access to 95% of the information at 95% of times (Bagchi 2005).

Freedom has been an important ingredient of India's success in IT. A well-developed and free *private corporate sector*, freedom of ideas, movement and political or religious affiliations are all offshoot of this basic element Freedom which nurtured under Indian democracy. Even in the socialism days, the private enterprise was allowed to grow freely. Mathur (2006) recognizes public-private partnership for growth of IT. Huang and Khanna (2003) commend India for improved corporate governance and fostering private sector development. For instance, India

---

[44]Religious-Historic epic Mahabharata also refers to the Unions and Republics which used to elect their leaders.
[45]International Herald Tribune (URL: http://www.iht.com/articles/2006/03/05/news/assess.php)
[46]Anyone who has lived in India knows that Indian press is the freest in the world.

has adopted public-private partnership in infrastructure development programs (Majumder 2006).

5.3. Education

The higher education miracle is something that India can be legitimately proud of.
~Jairam Ramesh[47].

Indian tradition is that of strong scientific and technical institutions and skills (Lema and Hesbjerg 2003). Education has always been in the core of the Indian culture. The Takshshila (600 BC) and Nalanda (400 BC) are two ancient Indian universities which were filled by the Indian and foreign students[48]. Long before and after these universities, there has been an ancient tradition of boarding schools system called Gurukul[49]. The tradition of excellent educational institutions was re-established after independence with Nehru's vision in favour of the higher education and training system. There has been a remarkable growth of Indian Education since India became a republic in 1950 (see Table 10). In the first twenty-five years after independence, the number of universities in India quadrupled, and the number doubled again over the next twenty-five years.

---

[47]Jairam Ramesh, Sect. of Congress Party, Economic Affairs department, has been a key player in developing India's 1991 economic reforms. Currently, he is a member of the National Advisory Council of India setup on June 4, 2004 by Prime Minister Manmohan Singh.
[48]Myanmar's Nobel laureate Aung San Suu Kyi, Afghan president Mr Hamid Karzai and Nepalese premier GP Koirala are among some foreign dignitaries who have studied in India.
[49]Unlike modern concept of education as a passport to better livelihood, Gurukul system of education was meant to achieve knowledge and was voluntarily managed and run by selfless scholars funded by the society without any interference or regulation from the administration. Indian children were initiated in education at the age of five and had to study until they turn 25. From 25 to 50 years of age, they were supposed to live a family life and earn money by ethical means and support the education system in form of donations to the Gurukuls. At the age of 50, they were supposed to act as visiting teachers of their respective trades in the Gurukuls.

Table 10: Quantitative Expansion

S. No	Item	Figure in 1950-51	Figure in 2003-04 (Unless otherwise stated)
1	Literacy Rate	18.3%	64.8% (2001)
2	Female Literacy Rate	8.9%	53.7%
3	Schools	0.23 million	1.18 million
4	General Colleges	370	9427
5	Professional Colleges	208	2751
6	Universities	27	304
7	Gross Enrolment Ratio in Elementary Education	32.1%	84.8%
8	Gender Parity Index at Elementary level	0.38	0.93
9	Public Spending on Education (% of GDP)	1.5%	3.76%

Source: http://www.education.nic.in/sector.asp#size

Only a select few countries could develop a technical education system comparable to the Indian Institutes of Technology (IITs) which later produced many internationally recognized IT leaders besides setting a high standard in education. Besides IITs, there is a very strong network of engineering and technological institutes, Regional Engineering Colleges and private sector educational institutions. As clear from the Figures 8 and 9, the numbers of engineering colleges and the engineering graduates are increasing every year.

Figure 7: Growth and Distribution of Intake in Degree (Engineering)

Source: HRD (2006)

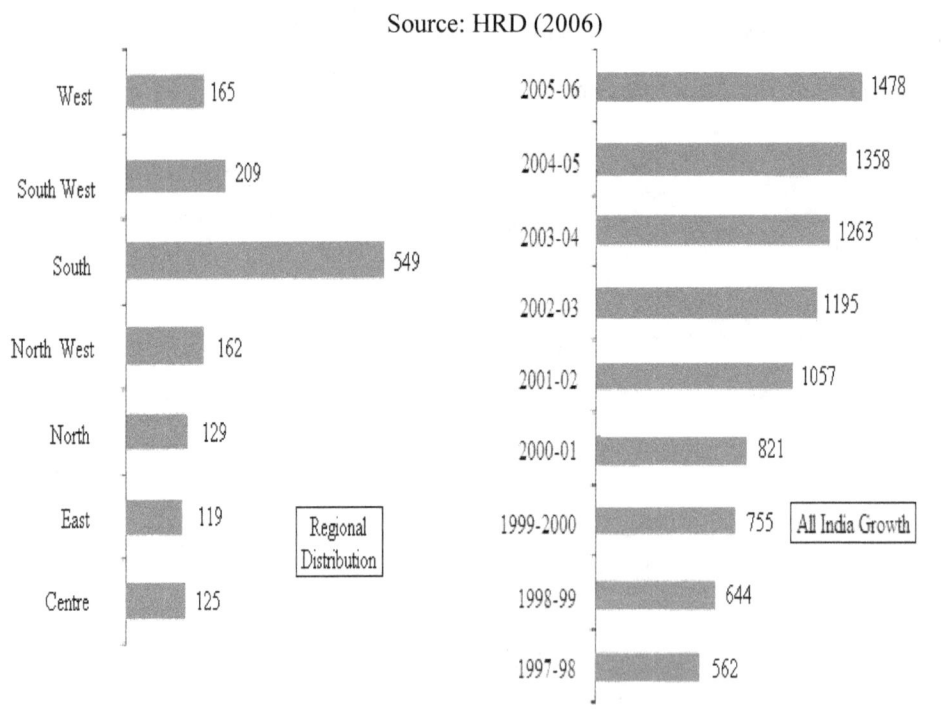

Figure 8: Growth and Distribution of Degree Colleges (Engineering)

Other strong educational institutions include the Indian Institutes of Management (IIM), and the Indian Institute of Science (IISc). With over 300 universities, 15,000 colleges, and 5,000 training institutions higher education system in India is extensive and rapidly expanding. The Indian education system prepared the students to fit the ever-changing world. By keeping itself abreast of market demands, it made the students capable of being ambitious and high achiever.

Besides formal college education, Indian IT and other industries have formal developmental and learning systems in place. There are libraries, plans for career path and a good number of hours of training per employee based on their needs. 98% of Indian companies have a formal training feedback mechanism (NASSCOM 2005b).

NASSCOM is working with the IT industry and Academia closely to keep the academia abreast of the skill set requirement of the industry including the expertise in non-technical areas like management and soft skills as well. It has signed a Memorandum of Understanding (MoU) with University Grants Commission (UGC) to jointly undertake a Faculty Development Program (FDP) to upgrade the skill-sets and knowledge base of the existing technical faculty in partnership with IT industry (NASSCOM 2006). The Indian society's love of education is one of its strongest points in getting unprecedented success in IT.

5.4. Karma (Action) and Kaal (Time)

The Indian philosophy revolves around the Karma or action which is the root of everything that happens around us and beyond. Karma is the cause of our particular destiny, the law of nature that ensures that we become what we think or do (Waterstone 1995).

Kaal or time is the cycle with no beginning and end. Combined with Hindu philosophy of rebirth, the concept of Kaal allows people to make plans spanned across the generations which may look slow but have a solid ground and long lasting effect In other words, Indian philosophy stresses on long-term goals as contrary to short-term gains.

Combined together, Karma and Kaal make a winning combination that produces a synergy which is steady and permanent though it may not be easily visible initially. This is exactly what happened in case of advanced technologies in India. The process was already in place and it is going to stay for a long time.

5.5. Diversity

Indian thoughts are not exclusive minded. They are ready to allow that there may be alternative approaches to the mystery. ~ Arnold Toynbee.

The idea of India is not based on language, geography, ethnicity, or religion. It is of one land embracing many (Tharoor 1997). There are 22 official 'scheduled' languages. The Ethnologue lists 428 Indian languages out of which 415 are living (Raymond 2005). India is an ocean and the Indian identity is a celebration of diversity. It is the original melting pot of cultures, ethnicities and ideas. Indians are comfortable with multiple identities and multiple loyalties, all coming together in allegiance to a larger idea of India, an India which safeguards the common space available to each identity, and an India that remains safe for diversity (Tharoor 1997). The idea of unity in diversity matures the vision of an average Indian with tolerance, respect and adjustments to differences and changes.

The exposure to diversity in everyday life, helps adjusting to a new business domain easily. It helps to change management practices effectively. It also provides a wider outlook to accommodate different views and opinions and accept the best available option globally. To be more precise, diversity helps Indians acquire a rare ability; overcoming false patriotism in favor of acquiring a quality which may be foreign.

5.6. Global Market

Could there be an industry without demand? The success of Indian IT industry puzzled some strategists because they virtually saw no domestic market. Athreye (2005) marks Indian IT industry as an export-led industry due to the predominance of exports. The success of Indian IT industry, in spite of little domestic demand explains an important attribute of the globalization: the market need not be divided into global and domestic. Furthermore, presence of a domestic market is no more a necessity for success of an industry. In other words, it is not that India was not ready; the fact is that the market was not ready for India. The success of Infosys is history today. Very few people know that before Infosys, N. R. Narayana Murthy started Softronics in 1976 which closed its operations after struggling for 16 months. He waited for the right time and founded Infosys with eyes at the global market. Hence, *global market* is an important ingredient of India's success in IT.

5.7. Language of Success

English is increasingly becoming the lingua franca of the IT. India today has the second-largest English-speaking scientific manpower pool in the world second only to the USA (Bajpai and Shastri 1998). General impression is that English has helped India to stay ahead of the competitors in an industry that speaks English. Besides being one of the official languages of India, English is the official language of two Indian states Meghalaya and Nagaland. It is taught as a second language throughout India except Bihar. India is the third largest English book-producing country after the United States and the United Kingdom. Times of India is among top five English news papers of the world. Familiarity with English is one such strength that has put India way ahead of competition in IT.

The question arises: is English central to this success? The answer is no! Indian software engineers are in demand in non-English speaking countries also. A major portion of the software market in India is dedicated to native languages. With growing Chinese and Indian economies, English may soon be replaced by an Asian language. Indian strength lies not in knowing English but in accepting and mastering a new or foreign language.

5.8. Economy, Efficiency and Lower Overall Cost

Indians are good in implementing strict cost controls and early warning systems in place. Though the supercomputers of C-DAC are at par with any North American, European or Japanese supercomputer, they are *more affordable* than any competition. In 2001, the scientists from the Indian Institute of Science in Bangalore in alliance with an Indian firm Encore developed Simputer with features of a personal computer. At approximately $200.00 each, the Simputer not only broke the $1000 barrier of the personal computer (PC) market, it was the cheapest ever.

In every single market you can retain market share through low base cost. India is being successful not because of lower direct cost but because of lower overall costs and high quality.

So, while China should not be underestimated, it will take time for it to achieve the kind of maturity that India has achieved ... India has a great deal to be proud of and must continue to focus[50] (Mike 2002). Getting cost saving without compromising quality is tough. For growth of IT industry too, it is lower overall cost that matters. The Indian IT sector beats other countries by providing world class IT solutions at a fraction of cost.

5.9. Human Resources

Dominance of knowledge economy over the old 'brick-and-mortar' economy is visible around the world. I am convinced that this is where the Indian advantage lies.
~ Manmohan Singh[51], Prime Minister of India.

Qualified human resources are the basic building blocks of Indian IT industry. IT industry requires various skill levels of human resources. With 16 percent of the world's population, India is the second most populous country on Earth. Indian pool of scientific and technical personnel is the third-largest in the world. India's superiority of human resource flourished in its long democratic tradition and education infrastructure. The combination of higher education system and the cultural traits provided India to develop the right kind of human resources for the IT. Skilled manpower is a key factor for the success of Indian software industry (Lakha 1994) and higher level of human capital enhances the regional growth (Mathur 1999). The strength of a nation's human capital stems from a multi-generational tradition of science and engineering and this strong human capital in software cannot emerge within a few years (Carmel 2003). A large network of the world class science, engineering, technical and management colleges is available to support this (see Table 11).

India is not complacent of the number of IT professionals. Steps such as IT Workforce Development Initiative launched by NASSCOM concentrate on creation and nurturing of the human resources as India moves towards a knowledge economy. In collaboration with the

---

[50]Mike Dodd, VP, Research Agenda, Giga Information Group as quoted in The Hindu Business Line (URL: http://www.thehindubusinessline.com/iw/2002/02/17/stories/2002021700080700.htm)
[51]Symmetry – May 2006 (URL: http://www.symmetrymagazine.org/cms/?pid=1000321)

industry, NASSCOM and UGC have undertaken the Faculty Development Program (FDP) to upgrade the skill sets and knowledge base of the existing technical faculty in India.

Table 11: Indian IT Sector Workforce

Workforce (in '000s)	2003-04	2004-05	2005-06E	2006-07E
Engineering Graduates	215	284	348	382
IT professionals (Computer Science, Electronics, Telecom)	141	165	181	193
IT professionals entering the workforce	80	94	103	109
Non-IT engineers entering the workforce	40	40	40	40
Graduates entering the IT workforce (other disciplines)	30	30	30	30
Total fresh IT Workforce	150	164	173	180

Source: NASSCOM

Not only India but USA too depends largely on human resources from India. Indians form the largest component of the employees coming to USA through specialty profession non-immigrant visa category H1. 30,000 visas were issued to Indians in 2005. The number of Indians coming to the USA for higher education is also on the rise recording an increase of 30 per cent in 2005. There are over 90,000 Indian students in USA. Many of these students are absorbed by US industry and a large number start their own companies. Indians were running only 3 percent of the technology companies started between 1980 and 1983 in Silicon Valley. The percentage increased to 10 between 1995 and 2000. The pace of Indian entrepreneurship accelerated rapidly in the 1990s. By 2000, Indians headed 972 technology companies (Saxenian 2002).

5.10. Competition as a Way of Life

Indians have adopted themselves to face competition[52] as a way of life. Competition is much tougher for admission in the engineering and management colleges and universities. The Joint Entrance Exam for admission in IITs is considered to be one of the toughest competitions in the world.

5.11. Strategic Location

The geographical location of India is a big advantage today. Being half way around the world from the USA translates to the optimum time differential when Indian engineers and call centres work while USA business people and doctors are sleeping. Outsourcing jobs to India enable the American companies to provide round-the-clock service and meet deadlines.

5.12. Law and Judiciary

India has a functional, efficient and independent judiciary. According to the World Economic Forum (WEF), India ranks 26 among 121 countries in judicial independence. China ranks much lower at 62 in the same report. Enforcement of the IT Act 2000 assures India's commitment to deal with cyber crimes and providing appropriate training to the law-enforcing agencies to handle such crimes. Recent amendments have made the Indian Copyright laws almost toughest in the world (Bajpai and Shastri 1998).

5.13. Established Financial System

With Reserve Bank of India as the central bank, India has a wide network of banking and other financial institutions. Though modern banking in India originated in the first decade of 18th century with The General Bank of India coming into existence in 1786 followed by Bank of Hindustan, indigenous banking is as old as Indian civilization. India has a large network of banks. Indian banks have efficiently played the role of social banking using tools such as micro-credit, priority sector loans and lead bank schemes. Now in their new reincarnation they are assisting the IT for its capital needs. While Non Performing Assets (NPA) is a top concern

---

[52]When I applied for the position of a probationary officer in a bank in 1987, over 600,000 people were short listed for the notoriously tough written exam followed by an interview.

in banks all over the world, the numbers are falling consistently in India. As a percentage of GDP, the Net NPA of Indian banks stood merely at 1.4% as on March 2006 as compared to 3.1% in 2004-05. As a percentage of GDP, gross NPA in India was just 1.9 % compared to 6.7% in China as on March 2005. As illustrated in Figure10, Indian banks ranked second in Asia in keeping the NPAs to a minimum.

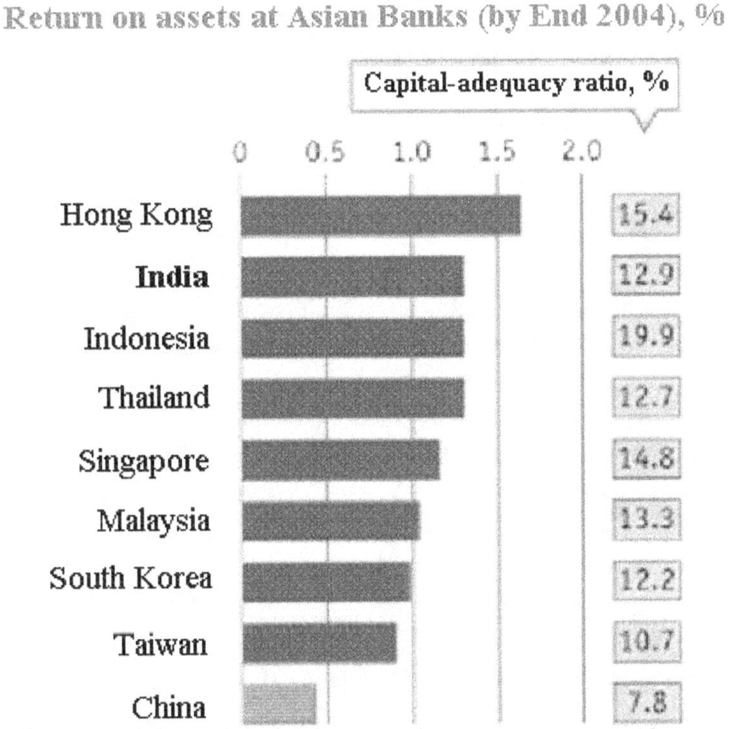

Return on assets at Asian Banks (by End 2004), %

Figure 9: NPAs among Asian Banks

Source: Fitch Institutions-Asia

5.14. Quality and Management Practices

India is now teaching the world about quality.
~Mike Dodd, VP, Research Agenda, Giga Information Group[53].

---

[53]*Business Line*
(URL: http://www.thehindubusinessline.com/iw/2002/02/17/stories/2002021700080700.htm)

Core competences allow firms to compete better than the average firm in their sector (Prahalad and Hamel 1990). India has the core competences required for the IT industry. Quality has been the magic mantra for Indian companies. The work culture of an Indian IT company can easily be defined by combining quality with best management practices. Starting from fixing Y2K bugs worldwide, India has become a leader in IT, ITeS and BPO industries. The journey has been smooth due to the superior management practices of Indian companies. Besides process maturity and quality, Indian IT industry has implemented the best Human Resource Management (HRM) systems in place to handle human resources issues such as recruiting, retaining and mentoring the best talent for the job.

5.14.1 Implementing Standards and Quality Controls

Indian IT industry climbed up the quality ladder very fast. They have been prompt in adapting to the world standard. Indian companies were early adopters of the ISO model. When the Capability Maturity Model (CMM) was proposed by the Software Engineering Institute (SEI)[54], Indian IT industry pioneered to fit the tough standards provided by the CMM proving their solid strength in project and process management.

When Motorola's Bangalore office acquired CMM Level 5 in 1994, it was second only to NASA. In June, 1999 Wipro of India became the first software services company in the world to attain SEI CMM maturity level 5, the highest maturity level. Every year many IT companies in the world enter into the CMMI regime or improve their CMMI Levels. As of 2006, about 75% of the CMMI level 5 software centers are in India.

India's pursuit of excellence in systems and methodologies is evident from BPO industry. Being a new area of business, BPO lacked any existing standards. NASSCOM and McKinsey recently developed a new benchmark called Process360° to help BPO operators identify key operational gaps using 14 operational areas.

---

[54]The Software Engineering Institute (SEI) is a federally funded research and development center sponsored by the U.S. Department of Defense and operated by Carnegie Mellon University, Pittsburgh, USA.

5.14.2 Acting Global

A new chapter was written in the history of the Indian industry when Infosys became the first Indian company to get listed on the NASDAQ in 1999. Other Indian companies followed Infosys. Eight Indian companies were listed in NYSE including Wipro, VSNL, Silverline, Satyam, Rediff and Sify. NASDAQ later opened an office in Bangalore.

Many companies are taking the quicker path of merger and acquisition (M&A) of the established companies overseas for specific advantage in terms of customer domain or geography. The total value of M&A and initial public offerings in the industry could touch $3-5 billion between 2005 and 2010, with large transactions grabbing a chunk of the pie, according to an Evalueserve[55] study.

Table 12: Some Acquisitions abroad by Indian IT Companies

Indian Company	Acquired Company
Patni Computers	Cymbal Corporation
Helios & Matheson	Maruthi Info Tech Inc
HTMT (Hinduja)	C3 (Philippines)
TCS	Incat International (UK)
Essar	Aegis Communications group (40% stake)
Essar	e-telequest
HTMT (Hinduja)	One Communications

Many companies are looking for alternatives to US and Europe. India's fourth-largest software company Satyam Computer Services Ltd. unveiled plans in December 2006 to set up a global software development center in Malaysia, and said it may open a similar campus in China.[56] Other IT giants such as TCS, Wipro and Infosys have already set up operations in China.

---

[55]Evalueserve (URL: http://www.evalueserve.com/Research/evs_Research.asp?q=qUKPR#).
[56]Yahoo India News (URL: http://in.news.yahoo.com/061207/210/6a3du.html)

5.14.3 Time Management

Hofstader's Law (Hofstadter 1979) states that software development always takes longer than you think. Indian Software Companies have a consistent track record of meeting deadlines. The sincerity and dedication in meeting the goals within the budget and time combined with the competence has been crucial in their success.

5.14.4 Reliability

"Close relationships in cyberspace, as in real life, can make either partner more vulnerable. A relationship, solely by virtue of the value it brings to its partners, may be attacked by the competitors of both. ~ Libicki (2006).

Indian companies have been proved to be reliable in outsourcing and for technology sharing. The government of India has taken serious steps to curb software piracy and to tackle the issues of hacking, data vulnerability and identity theft by replacing its dated laws with new acts such as Information Technology Act 2000 with strong prohibitions regarding data theft.

5.14.5 Learning Organizations

India will become the knowledge production centre with highest intellectual capital per dollar. ~ R.A. Mashelkar, Director General, CSIR, India.[57]

A Learning organization is able to anticipate change and become more effective by acquiring new skill sets. Employee empowerment is as important in a learning organization as group collaboration. Learning organizations learn through the synergy of the individual learners (Senge 1990). Not only the Indian IT Companies are taking definitive steps in evolving into Learning Organizations, they have an annual summit to select the India's "Most Admired Knowledge Enterprises" (MAKE). The annual Indian MAKE study serves as a benchmark to recognize Indian companies which are leaders in effectively transforming enterprise knowledge into wealth-creating ideas, products and solutions. One of the clearest metrics to demonstrate

---

[57]Times Of India. February 6, 2004 (URL: http://timesofindia.indiatimes.com/articleshow/478156.cms)

this fact is Total Shareholder Return (TSR). Last year, the TSR for the 2006 Indian MAKE winners was 28%, more than five times that of the US Fortune 500 company median 5.4%.[58].

5.14.6 Knowledge Management

The illiterate of this century will not be those who cannot read and write, but those who cannot learn, unlearn, and relearn. ~ Alvin Toffler

Companies need to invest in training their employees - both in technology as well as other management aspects. To compete in today's knowledge economy we need to empower the people with knowledge. Indian firms have taken several proactive measures to increase productivity (Murthy 2003). The Indian IT companies have invested heavily in knowledge management. They have created robust knowledge management infrastructure and developed tools to increase productivity and reusability.

5.14.7 Collaborations, Alliances and Partnerships

The central and state governments in India realized the power of collaborations, alliances and partnerships at an early stage. Same is true about private sectors in India. The main path of Indian companies' entry into the US and other foreign markets has been through strategic alliance and partnerships with foreign companies.

Sankhya Vahini India Limited (SVIL) was proposed as a joint venture between the Government and IUNet[59] in 1998. The goal was to provide 10,000 km of multi-pair fiber-optic network. Though the project did not get clearance from the Indian parliamentary Standing Committee on Communications for legal reasons, it certainly paved way for later collaborations.

E-Chaupal is a joint venture of the government of Andhra Pradesh and the Indian Tobacco Company (ITC) as a public-private partnership initiative through Farmer's Friends groups for the chili and turmeric producing farmers (Manohar 2005). Numerous other collaborative efforts

---

[58]Bharti Airtel Media Center Recent Highlights, FY2006-2007 (URL:
http://www.bhartiairtel.in/182.0.html?&tx_ttnews%5Btt_news%5D=360&tx_ttnews%5BbackPid%5D=1&cHash=0eb8ee552d.
[59]A subsidiary of Carnegie Mellon University (CMU) in Pittsburgh, USA

are taking place throughout India and abroad involving Indian industry, government institutions or NGOs ultimately resulting in the betterment of Indian society.

5.14.8 Networking through Diaspora

On December 10, 2006, astronaut Sunita Williams soared into space toward the International Space Station for six months. She is the second woman of Indian origin to achieve this glorious place after Kalpana Chawla. Be it Nobel laureates S. Chandrashekhar and Dr. Hargobind Khurana, musicians Ravi Shankar[60] and Pt. Vishwa Mohan Bhatt[61] or entrepreneurs Indira Nooyi[62] and Amar Gopal Bose[63], the diaspora has always made Indians proud.

Indian government and private sectors recognize the importance of Indian diaspora in gaining new grounds in IT. Ministry of Overseas Indian Affairs (MOIA) is working[64] to create synergy between industry and diaspora. Some companies in Silicon Valley, like Sun Microsystems, run by Indian national Vinod Khosla, have partnered with Indian firms for software development or other production processes, thus alleviating the effects of brain drain[65]. The homecoming of Sam Pitroda and Sabeer Bhatia[66] was considered as brain gain as contrary to brain drain.

---

[60]He has 14 honorary doctorates and prestigious awards from across the globe including, the Padma Vibhushan, the Magsaysay Award, three Grammy Awards, and the Crystal Award from Davos, with the title "Global Ambassador". His daughter Norah Jones too won several Grammy Awards, and selling 20 million albums.
[61]He was awarded a Grammy award for Best World Music Album in 1994.
[62]First lady CEO of Pepsi
[63]The chairman and founder of Bose Corporation
[64]MOIA formed a committee on the Indian diaspora in 2000. Annual Pravasi Bhartiya Divas (PBD) is organized as a festival of the diaspora by the MOIA in partnership with the Confederation of Indian Industry (CII) and the Delhi government. MOIA's Know India Program (KIP) 2006-07 will involve a total of three weeks stay in India for 30 participants consisting of emigrant youth professionals and students of the age group of 20-28 years.
[65]Source: Stanford Journal of International Relations
(URL: http://www.stanford.edu/group/sjir/6.1.05_nagala.html)
[66]Sabeer Bhatia created Hotmail which was later acquired by Microsoft

5.14.9 Ethics

Ethics is another highlight of the new generation of Indian business. This is a major shift from the businesses of the past. The new leadership does not believe Union Carbide[67], Google[68] or Enron way of business and they are ready to pay a higher price for the values they respect. According to Narayana Murthy[69], "you cannot compartmentalize different ethics in business and personal life...It may translate to paying a certain cost for your belief... The value system is tested in at the moment of adversity, in difficult times and not when everything is going well." Horowitz (2003) supports this view while stating that the businesses that will be around for the long term are those that put honesty, integrity, and quality at the top of their list, that stake their marketing strategy on building positive long-term relationships with not just customers, but also employees, suppliers, and even competitors.

5.14.10 Commitment to Quality

In the initial days, some sceptics dismissed the Indian success as a temporary phase resulting from cheap labour. They failed to understand that many countries with cheaper labour and better infrastructure could not create this success. One important factor for India's success is the commitment to quality. Traditional Indian outlook is different from the rest of the world in the sense that it develops passion for quality without expectation, incentives and attachment. Indian IT companies paid extra attention to the quality of work and have moved up the value chain. After proving their excellence in low-cost outsourcing jobs they shifted towards software services and developed organizational and managerial capabilities that enabled them to offer more comprehensive services. Today, most Indian firms are developing stronger strategic partnership instead of just outsourcing partnership with foreign companies.

---

[67]Over 4000 people were killed and many more suffered due to a gas leak in Union Carbide plant in Bhopal because the company insisted on cost-cutting measures without caring for human lives.
[68]To do business in China, Google agreed to censor its results through www.google.cn.
[69]An interview with Dr Prannoy Roy on NDTV on December 22, 2006.

5.14.11 Decision Making

Indians believe in democratic processes and structures. They spend more time to analyze and discuss every aspect of a deal before making a decision. Once a decision is made, entire team including the disapprovers commit to it. Decisions are announced by the top of the hierarchy as the seniority is highly respected in India.

5.14.12 Customer Oriented Approach

Cultural compatibility and friendly customer relationship is a significant success factor for the Indian IT and ITeS companies. They value their client and spend a fair amount of time in understanding the requirements before moving on to build and deliver quality product or service[70]. Instead, they believe in winning the customer through excellent service. India did not lose a dime when IBM refused to accept FERA and left India. It was IBM that lost a big future market. They are back now but the message is clear, "The customer is supreme".

5.14.13 Senior Management

The quality of the senior management in Indian companies has been a big plus. Indian IT management is very proficient in setting clear, measurable goals, monitoring day-to-day progress, persistently removing obstacles, and delivering the goods within deadlines. Names like Narayana Murthy have become legendry in IT industry. "India's greatest competitive advantage is not merely the large number of talented developers, but even more the large number of senior executives who understand how and why to run a high maturity organization" (Bill Curtis[71] as quoted in Dataquest[72]).

---

[70]Compare mobile phone market in India and USA. Unlike USA, no contracts are needed in India. No locked phones, no additional charges for value added services like SMS etc., and no airtime charges for inward calls. And all of this for a fraction of the cost compared to USA. Indian companies know that they cannot keep charging ridiculously high fees to the customers for a long time.

[71]Dr. Bill Curtis is a former Director of the Software Process Program at the Software Engineering Institute (SEI) at CMU Pittsburgh.

[72]Dataquest (URL: http://www.dqindia.com/content/advantage/103102703.asp)

5.14.14 Innovation

India might not be a mass producer and it may never become the factory of the world. India is artistic and innovative. With products like Bancs2000, Infosys started innovating in 1989. Indian companies used the software technology skills to drive technology-based products too. The new technology framework, VirtualWorks developed by Ramco Systems, is an example of this type of product (Krishnan and Prabhu 1999). The MNCs are coming forward to cash India's strength in this area. Lenovo is launching its first Innovation Centre in India, in partnership with Intel, Microsoft, LANDesk, IBM and Cisco. Many Indian companies are already innovative world beaters (Elliott 2006).

5.15. Success through Leadership

> *"Unlike the West, where things are more homogenous, India has a diverse culture. Hence, it has a good potential to develop good leaders. Indians grow up learning to collaborate and viewing things differently." ~ Mike R. Jay*[73]

Jawaharlal Nehru, India's first prime minister, is the founding father of the tradition of education, science, technology and industrial development of modern India. The new IT leaders like Narayana Murthy played an important role in bringing India to where it stands today. Institutions like NASSCOM and IBEF have played very important role in building India as a global brand. Our survey provided a list of people who are considered as leaders in India's success in IT. Profiles of some of the visionaries who need special mention in this regard are listed in Appendix F.

5.15.1 A new trend

> *The US has discovered India's high-tech industry, and the credit is largely due to shy, unflappable engineer N.R. Narayana Murthy. ~ Business Week (1999).*

The culture of IT companies in India is entirely different from the traditional businesses and so is their leadership. Most of these IT businesses are started by a new generation of educated people from middle class families without any business experience as contrary to the

---

[73]Leadership in India (URL: http://generati.typepad.com/mrj/2006/05/leadership_in_i.html)

established business houses such as Tata, Birla, Malya, Ambani, Goenka, Jains etc. Kapur (2002) endorses this view and states that most of the (IT) success stories were scripted by the first generation entrepreneurs, who were not born in a family of millionaires. This new generation is full of ideas and ideals, dreams and visions, ambition and generosity. In 1993, Mr. Narayana Murthy of Infosys made a public vow that Infosys would strive to make a hundred employees millionaires by the year 2000. It was unheard of that an entrepreneur would evaluate his success or the success of the enterprise based on how much wealth it could create for people who work for the organization (Bagchi 2005).

The old school of business while blaming the government for controls and regulation, abused the system by cheating on every front including quality of products, taxes and the payments of dues for power and other utilities. Some used unfair means including bribes, muscle power and collusion with corrupt bureaucrats, police and politicians to pollute the environment and silence the whistleblowers. The black economy has been a major concern for India. This parallel economy is estimated to account for 25-50% of India's GDP[74]. IT revolution led the way for the new wave of companies like MindTree, Wipro and Infosys which live by the principles of complete transparency and integrity down the organization. These are articulated and evangelized by the top management (Bagchi 2005).

5.15.2 NASSCOM

The creation of India's National Association of Software and Service Companies (NASSCOM) as a not-for-profit organization in 1988 with 38 members indicated India's readiness for the IT challenge. It is the premier trade body and the chamber of commerce of the IT software and services industry in India. NASSCOM is a global trade body with over 1,050 members, of which over 150 are global companies from the US, UK, EU, Japan and China. NASSCOM's member companies are in the business of software development, software services, software products and IT-enabled/BPO services.

---

[74]Financial Express
(URL: http://www.financialexpress.com/columnists/full_column.php?content_id=145293)

NASSCOM's vision is to establish India as the 21st century's software powerhouse and position the country as the global sourcing hub for software and services. It has been the strongest proponent of global free trade in India. NASSCOM is working proactively to encourage its members to adopt world class management practices, build and uphold highest quality standards and become globally competitive.

5.15.3 IBEF

The India Brand Equity Foundation (IBEF) is a public-private partnership run jointly by the Ministry of Commerce & Industry and the Confederation of Indian Industry to create and develop a positive brand identity for India and make the "Made in India" and "Served from India" brands as symbols of quality, reliability and service. IBEF has represented Indian industry under a banner globally as a reliable supplier of quality goods and services.

5.16. Success through Government Policies

The presence of a national strategy for software exports is to be recognised as a vital part of software export success (Balasubramanyam & Balasubramanyam 1997). India has become the technology tiger it is today due to the policies Indian government adopted after independence, beginning with a big state-funded push, to educate scientists, educators and engineers. When India abandoned socialism in favour of free-market economy and the Indian telecommunications providers made sure high-bandwidth Internet access was available, the rest was history (Gibson 2005).

The successive policy reforms facilitated the emergence of an export oriented software industry in India the 1980s when body-shoppers sent the Indian programmers to work at the client sites in the USA, Singapore and Europe. According to Saxenian (2001), the shift to offshore production, allowing the programmers to work at facilities in India, became possible after the policy reforms of the early 1990s, especially the removal of licenses on imports of industrial equipment and the establishment of the STPs. These policies and their effects are discussed in detail in next chapter.

5.17. Summary

Besides low wages and English language, the recent economic reforms are generally credited for the IT growth. But there is lot more to India's success in IT. Diversity, education and cultural values provided the capability and confidence to Indian IT industry. The role of government policies and the management practices proved to be other attributes of this success. The character of new IT leadership and its pursuits of the toughest standards also play important role in this success. India has a long history of bravely facing all odds and learning from bad times and the failures to get stronger every time. Be it about learning Persian or English or switching from wearing Dhoti to Sherwani[75] to a three piece suite, Indians have been very adaptive without losing their core strengths of critical thinking, innovation, learning, knowledge and debates in the process.

---

[75]A long coat-like garment worn in India.

6.   SUCCESS THROUGH GOVERNMENT POLICIES

When countries create the right conditions - including openness to new investment and new ideas - they can recapture some of what they have lost. The Indians in Silicon Valley are an important part of Bangalore's success. ~ Nancy Birdsall[76] (2002)

There has always been a debate between the role played by the government and the private sector in development of any sector of economy. This question becomes more important while analyzing IT sector in India for following reasons:

- India has been a regulated socialistic economy for several decades.

- India's success in a high-tech sector such as IT is unprecedented for a developing country.

This chapter analyses India's economic background and the events that were crucial in creating the stage to groom and nurture India to be where it is now.

6.1. Pre-Independence

There is a land which is one of the garden spots of the globe; a land with a history dating back four thousand years, having boundless wealth... She was in her splendour when our forefathers were half-naked savages in English forests. Her scholars were writing great epics, and calculating eclipses... King Solomon borrowed some of her superfluities to increase the glory of his capital. ~ William Butler (1885).

Ancient Indian civilization was fairly advanced in mathematics, astronomy, literature, music, arts, architecture and philosophy besides trade and banking[77]. "In 1715, Indians accounted for 25 percent of world industrial output, so it's always been an industrial nation in that sense of the term" (Ramesh[78] 2001).

---

[76]Nancy Birdsall is a special adviser to the administrator of UNDP

[77]For instance, India was the only miner and supplier of the world's diamond for thousands of years until 18th century when diamonds were first mined outside India. No wonder that India was the richest country on earth until the time of European invasion.

[78]Jairam Ramesh was *a key player in developing India's 1991 economic reforms*

6.2. Rebirth of an Ancient Nation – Nehru's Socialistic Vision

When Nehru took charge of free India as the first prime minister, India was suffering from the massive refugee resettlement problem[79] besides economic disruptions and inadequate resources. Outbreak of the undeclared war over Kashmir added insult to injury. Nehru and much of the Indian independence movement were committed to industrialization of India. They wanted the state to play an active role. For them, independence meant independence from foreign capital, because their experience of capitalism was British capital owning bits of India. Nehru had started working on it about 10 years before independence (Desai[80] 2000). With help of legendry scientists and economists such as Mahalanobis[81], he provided first five year plan for the nation which was highly influenced by the Socialistic model.

Nehru laid the foundation for modern India with a strong foundation in education. He started IITs and institutes of sciences, management and other higher learning. India had no tax and zero import duties on books and periodicals. From day one, from 1947, the government of India released foreign exchange for students to go out and study abroad. Next sections discuss some of the fundamental planning decisions that became the basis for the success of today.

6.3. Planning Commission

Indian leadership adopted the principle of formal economic planning soon after independence as an effective way to intervene in the economy to foster growth and social justice. Planning Commission was established in 1950. The commission drafts national plans to be approved by the National Development Council[82], which can make changes in the draft plan. After approval, the draft is presented to the cabinet and subsequently to Parliament, whose approval makes the plan an operating document.

---

[79]Indian partition in 1947 resulted into the world's largest population transfer.
[80]Lord Meghnad Desai is a professor at the London School of Economics and director of the Center for the Study of Global Governance.
[81]A scientist and an economist Prasanta Chandra Mahalanobis gave the concept of the Mahalanobis distance in 1936. He founded National Sample Survey in 1950. He became the Honorary President of the International Statistical Institute in 1957.
[82]The National Development Council consists of the Planning Commission and the state chief ministers.

6.4. Five Year Plans

The First Five-Year Plan (1951-55) attempted to stimulate balanced economic development. The recent plans gave lot of thrust to IT without being a hindrance to its growth. The tenth plan document pledges to continue the Government's hitherto hands-off policy with regard to the IT sector in the Tenth Plan where the government will confine itself to being a facilitator and a catalyst for accelerated growth of the sector. It plans to take major initiatives in the area of e-governance with a view to ensuring balanced and orderly growth (Planning Commission: Tenth Five Year Plan 2002-2007).

6.5. Language Policy

A large pool of English speaking population is considered to be a major strength of India. The government policy of linguistic reorganization of Indian states played an important role in making English parallel to Hindi, the official language of India. In the late 1950's when language policy became a divisive issue, Nehru assured that English would enjoy the status of a parallel official language. This was the birth of the three language formula[83] of Indian education system. It developed a large pool of human capital capable of using English that helped India adapt IT in initial years and compete globally in IT and ITeS later.

Countries like China have recognized the success of India's language policy. While this book is being written[84], China's education minister Zhou Ji is in India visiting local universities and schools in search of language teachers to meet the growing demand for English in China. He is arranging tie-ups with Indian universities and institutes for English teachers to go to China to teach Chinese students and Chinese students to visit Indian schools[85]. Japan too has shown interest in inviting English teachers from India[86].

---

[83]Three language formula provides exposure to three languages in schools, a state/regional language, Hindi and English. State funded schools in Tamilnadu use bilingual formula where Hindi is not taught.
[84]Zhou Ji was in India in December 2006.
[85]BigNews.com (URL: http://feeds.bignewsnetwork.com/?sid=53368)
[86]CNN-IBN (URL: http://www.ibnlive.com/article.php?id=7601&section_id=3)

Rudolph (2000) suggests that India should continue multilingual education. The country as a whole will benefit if India's globally-oriented business, and not just IT, can continue to communicate with, and contribute to, the "wired" world of English.

6.6. Education Policy

IT is a knowledge based industry. Jobs in the IT field are varied, complex, and specialized, as are the knowledge, skills, and experience required to perform them. Employers seek workers who possess a specific combination of technical skills and experience, often coupled with a college degree, soft skills, and business or industry knowledge (US Department of Commerce 2003).

India's commitment to spread education among its citizens is reflected in its Constitution. Besides, the union and the state governments have articulated various legislations. Some of the important federal legislations on education are listed in Appendix C. The success of India's education policy reflects by the fact that within a few years of independence, India emerged as one of the largest Higher Education Systems in the world. According to the National Policy of Education website[87], there were 10 million students in 16,885 colleges being taught by approximately 457,000 teachers in 2005. There are about 888 thousand educational institutions in the country with an enrolment of about 179 millions. Elementary Education System[88] in India is the second largest in the World with 149.4 millions children of 6-14 years enrolled and 2.9 million teachers. This is about 82% of the children in the age group. Regional languages are the medium of instruction at the primary stage of education in most of the States. Teaching of English is compulsory in all the States, except Bihar.

6.7. IT Policy

As we saw in section 2.4, the government of India has been very pro-active in devising and implementing an effective IT policy. To avoid repetition, we shall have a quick look at the chronology of important policy milestones in the Table 13.

---

[87]National Policy of Education website (URL: http://education.nic.in/NatPol.asp#pol)
[88]There are over 200 school education working days in a year.

Table 13: Major Policy Events in Indian IT Scene

Year	Event
1966	Electronics Committee Report
1968	National Conference on Electronics
1970	Department of Electronics (DOE) established
1971	Electronics Commission established
1971	Information, Planning and Analysis Group (IPAG)
1975	National Informatics Centre (NIC) established
1976	CMC formed
1984	New Computer Policy
1984	CDoT started under Sam Pitroda
1986	Software Technology Parks of India
1986	Videsh Sanchar Nigam Limited (VSNL)
1986	Mahanagar Telephone Nigam
1988	CDAC formed
1988	Satellite based NICNET
1990	Software Technology Parks of India
1991	Indian economic liberalization begins
1997	Telecommunications Regulatory Authority of India (TRAI)
1998	National Task Force on IT & Software Development
1998	Education and Research Network
2000	IT Act
2001	CMC disinvested – Bought by Tata Group

6.8. National Informatics Centre

In the 1970s, the Electronics Commission and the Department of Electronics (DOE) forwarded a proposal to United Nations Development Program (UNDP) to set up the National Informatics Centre (NIC). The UNDP team visited India to study the proposal in March 1975. In 1978, the NIC started functioning as a system with the provision of detailed information management for the government and its agencies to assist them in making decisions relating to the country's economic and social development planning and program implementation.

6.9. The Pitroda Era

An electrical engineer by education, Sam Pitroda returned to India in the year 1984 to start the Center for Development of Telematics (CDoT). He later became advisor to the Prime Minister of India on National Technology Missions.

Using the novel concept of Public Call Office, he provided public access to telephones. He revolutionized the state of telecommunications in India by bringing telephones to some of the previously isolated regions. In the field of telecom, his emphasis was on accessibility rather than density. He holds over 50 patents and has lectured extensively on telecom, technology and development in almost all parts of the world[89]. More information on him can be found in Appendix F.

6.10. The Era of Indian Economic Liberalization

> *Despite of substantial borrowings from the IMF in July 1990 and January 1991 and a very severe import compression, foreign exchange reserves had been reduced to no more than two weeks worth imports.*
> *~Dr. Manmohan Singh (Prime Minister and Ex. Chairman Reserve Bank of India)*

The Indian Economic Liberalization may be said to set foot in 1991 when due to the Gulf war, the price of petroleum skyrocketed. The tightly controlled Indian economy was not able to handle the crisis well. Then chairman of the Reserve Bank of India Dr Manmohan Singh[90] is considered to be the charioteer of the economic liberalization. The liberalization process gave an instant boost to Indian economy including IT sector.

6.11. Taxation Incentives

India has a well developed tax structure which has undergone considerable reform in the past few years. Tax rates have been rationalized and the laws simplified. Tax revenue as a percentage of GDP has been consistently increasing. The Indian government offers many incentives to investors in India to promote growth and development. A ten year tax holiday is available to ventures engaged in infrastructure facility, power, notified industrial parks and special economic zones. There is also a five-year tax holiday for new industrial units set up in backward states and districts. These incentives have boosted the growth of IT industry in India. Thanks to the incentives, over 6,000 businesses are registered under the STPI scheme.

---

[89]Indobase: Indians Abroad: Sam Pitroda
(URL: http://www.indobase.com/indians-abroad/sam-pitroda.html)
[90]Eminent economist Dr. Manmohan Singh is current Prime Minister of India.

6.12. Other Incentives to the IT Industry

Other measures to support the IT industry include the simplification of the filing of Software Export Declaration Form (SOFTEX) and the acquisition of overseas parent-company shares by employees, stock options to non-resident and permanent-resident employees and foreign exchange remittance for buying services. Indian direct investment in joint-venture (JV)/wholly owned subsidiaries abroad was simplified and a fast-track window was made available. India made significant reforms in the area of intellectual property rights (IPRs), and joined the WTO. Trade related aspects of IPR policy reforms in the telecom sector helped accelerate the domestic and export industry. In 2002, international long-distance was liberalized two years ahead of WTO commitments and competition increased in cellular markets. As a result, India's tele-density[91] increased to five, and cellular penetration overtook the landline penetration.

Recognizing the growing need for manpower in the software industry, the Ministry of Human Resources Development took the following actions:

- Created and expanded the computer-science departments in existing engineering colleges.

- Encouraged private sectors to open a large number of engineering colleges.

- Introduced quality-control systems for engineering colleges and other IT-training institutions, such as the All India Council for Technical Education and accreditation system run by professional bodies, such as the Computer Society of India, to monitor private training institutions.

- Encouraged the private sector to open training institutions. At its peak, nearly 1 million Indians were being trained in a year with no government subsidy.

6.13. Ministry of Communications & Information Technology (MC&IT)

The MC&IT envisages IT providing a unique and new opportunity to improve the economic status of all sections of society. The vision also perceives IT addressing age-old problems in the fields of education, health, rural development, poverty alleviation, employment, etc., and being

---

[91]Tele-density is the number of phones per 100 people.

a major facilitator for information transparency, good governance, empowerment, participative management and grassroots democracy (Bajwa 2003).

6.14. National Task Force on IT & Software Development (NTFITSD)

The NTFITSD was set up by the Prime Minister's Office on May 22, 1998, under the Chairmanship of the Deputy Chairman of Planning Commission. This taskforce had a mandate to formulate the draft of a National Informatics Policy. It is a high powered group that included senior representatives from the private sector, government, and universities. It included the Executive Director of NASSCOM, senior executives from Infosys and Wipro, and a range of other scientists, professionals, educators, and military officials besides the Secretaries of the Departments including Electronics, Finance, Commerce, and Telecommunications (Saxenian 2001).

The NTFITSD set up four working groups, on IT Research, Design and Development, IT Human Resources Development, Citizen-IT Interface, and Content Creation and Content Industry each. It later developed an unusually open and transparent process for collecting information and formulating recommendations in consultation with various public and private-sector stakeholders. It released the Information Technology Action Plan (ITAP) in 1999 which was a major step in India's advancement in the area of IT.

6.15. Information Technology Action Plan (ITAP)

The ITAP is the most ambitious IT-related policy proposal in India since the Computer Policy of 1984 and the Software Policy of 1986. The Plan lists 108 recommendations of "revisions and additions to the existing policy and procedures for removing bottlenecks and achieving a pre-eminent status for India." And it sets as targets for 2008, $50 billion in software exports and "IT penetration for all."

6.16. Information Technology Act 2000 (ITA-2000)

The ITA-2000 provided the legal infrastructure for e-commerce in India. The Act legalizes the authentication and verification of electronic record by affixing digital signature. The Act details about Electronic Governance and regulation of the certifying authorities for digital certificates. The Act talks about penalties and adjudication for various computer related offences including cyber crimes and the establishment of the Cyber Regulations Appellate Tribunal and the Cyber Regulations Advisory Committee, which shall advice the government as regards any rules, or for any other purpose connected with the said act.

6.17. Software Technology Parks of India (STPI)

STPI was established in 1990 as an autonomous wing of the MCIT with an objective to promote the growth of the software industry. Figure 11 shows these parks on India's map. Following are some of the salient features of the STPI (Courtesy: STPI Mohali):

- Approvals are given under Single Window Clearance Mechanism
- 100% Foreign Equity is permitted
- All the imports in the STP units are completely duty free
- Import of Goods on loan, free of cost & lease basis is permitted
- Re-export of Capital Goods brought on loan/lease/free of cost is permitted
- Domestic purchases are completely excise duty free and eligible for the benefit of deemed exports to the suppliers
- The sales in Domestic Tariff Area (DTA) are permissible up to 50% of the value of Exports
- STP units are exempted from corporate income tax up to Year 2010.

Figure 10: Software Technology Parks of India

The offshore software exports from the country during 1991-92, grew to more than 90% from a mere 20-35% contributing to 95% of national software companies from STPI member companies.

6.18. Electronics Hardware Technology Park

Success of the STPI inspired the concept of the Electronics Hardware Technology Park (EHTP) to boost manufacturing electronics hardware in the country. The EHTP strategy is also 100% export-oriented for undertaking manufacture of electronic hardware equipment/components and other items. An EHTP may be set up by the central or state governments, public or private sector or any combination thereof. Interestingly, an EHTP unit may be an individual unit or a unit located in an area designated as an EHTP.

6.19. Summary

Conventional explanations of India's success failed because they ignored the role of the government. Kapur (2002) suggests that it is wrong to conclude that the state played no role in this success. The Indian state's much maligned trade and industrial policies had inadvertent positive effects for this sector (Kapoor 2002). The promotional role of the Indian state from 1984 is recognized by many scholars (Evans 1995, Saxenian 2001) as central in India's success. The long ignored role of earlier policy decisions is equally important in creating the right conditions for India to evolve as an Information superpower.

Since independence, the state envisioned Bangalore as the city of the future by developing scientific industries and research institutions in public sector which later pioneered India's IT success. Planning Commission, Five Year Plans, Language Policy and Education Policy helped the overall growth of the economy with a slow but steady pace. Socialistic policies helped developing a large network of education, banking and industrial network to the remotest places in India. The government action in 1977 led to the birth of domestic software industry. From IT Policy, NIC and CDoT to MC&IT and ITA-2000, the state kept molding the path of success for IT. The liberalization of the economy and concrete steps such as establishment of the STPI sped up the growth. Government and the public sector industries also helped the IT grow by being the largest consumer for very long time. Thus we see that the government has played important roles in building India as an IT superpower. These roles varied from visionary, custodian, manufacturer, promoter and consumer.

7. THE SUCCESS MODEL

There is abundance of literature explaining India's legendry success in IT. The quality of literature varies from superficial reports to scholarly models that go deep inside the Indian IT industry. This chapter investigates some of the existing models and background elements. It raises a few important questions. Can these models explain the success of IT in India? If not, why did they fail to predict India's success? Finally, it proposes a new model, the Indian Information Technology Success model (IITS) to explain India's success in IT. This model is tested for reusability for other industries and other countries.

7.1. SWOT[92] Analysis

Strengths and Weaknesses are internal to an organization while Opportunities and Threats are external. Table 14 lists the SWOT components for Indian IT industry envisioned by many scholars, business entrepreneurs, policy makers etc. Chapters 4 and 5 discussed the weaknesses and the strengths of the Indian IT sectors in depth. GDM helped India excel in IT as in a closed world excellence may not be enough to become a world leader. The threats of cheap labour may be handled by controlling the overall costs and providing a package of the services. Political opposition[93] in western countries is not India's headache. A likely slowdown in demand can be countered by increasing demand in newer areas and also in domestic sector.

Promoting English in other countries is not an issue for India because the question is not about English. The Indian strength lies in the adaptability and the openness towards languages. India's linguistic diversity makes it easier to learn a foreign language which may be difficult for people from nations with just one or two languages. Also, the language of business changes with time. The way Chinese economy is growing, combined with the growth of Macau, Hong Kong and Taiwan, Chinese may soon replace English or for a second thought, India being the

---

[92]SWOT is an acronym for strengths, weaknesses, opportunities, and threats.
[93]Ultimately, the businesses in these countries will have to choose between growth and short-sightedness. In the global economy, any country that covers its business by protection, subsidies or regulations will end up hurting its own interests.

back office of the world, some Indian languages may eventually become the business language of tomorrow. Besides, low level programming languages are not dependent on any human language be it English or German.

Table 14: SWOT of Indian IT Industry

Strengths	Weaknesses
India brand advantage Language advantage Government Support and policies Overall Cost advantage Skilled workforce Expertise in new technologies BPO & Call center leadership Leverage relationships in West to access overseas markets Indian domestic-market growth	Poverty and Financial Disparity Illiteracy Corruption, greed and tolerance for unethical behavior Nepotism, Job Reservations and Cheap Politics Economic Patriotism
Opportunities	**Threats**
Global Delivery Model MNC leveraging India advantage Economy	A likely slowdown in demand Cheap labor in other countries Initiatives to learn English by other countries Political opposition in Western countries like the United States

7.2. Porter's Diamond Model

Porter's Diamond Model (Porter 1998) for the competitive advantage of Nations for a specific industry or cluster helps us to understand the comparative position of a nation in global competition. As depicted in Figure 12, it is based on six factors (four determinants and two non-determinants) of national competitive advantage and their interaction with each-other. The four determinants listed below are bi-directional and influence each other:

- Factor Conditions

- Demand Conditions

- Related and Supporting Industries

- Structure, Strategy and Rivalry of the Firm/Industry.

.The non-determinant factors are "Chance" and "Government" which influence the four determinant factors. All six factors need not be optimal for firms or clusters to be successful. Diamond model stresses that the factors influence each other and reliance on any one factor is unsustainable over time.

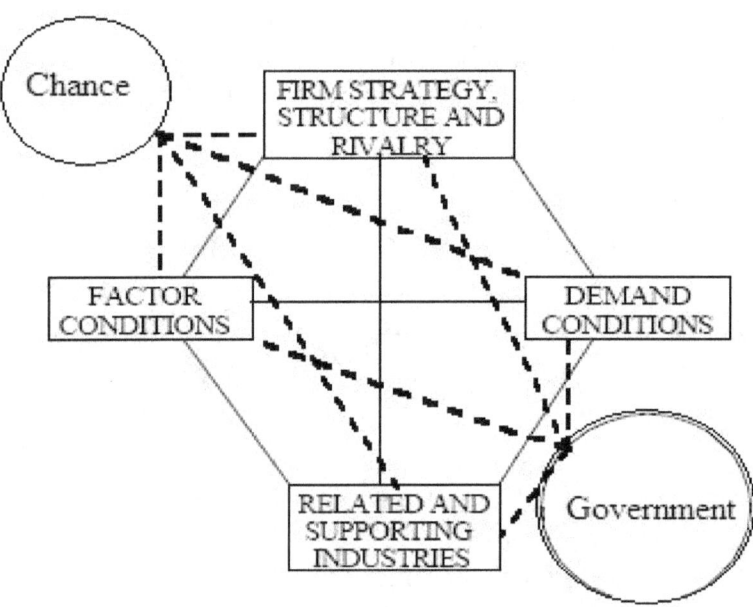

Figure 11: Porter's Diamond Model of Competitive Advantage of Nations

The next step is to test Diamond model for India's success in IT. Chapter 6 discussed the first non-determinant factor "Government" in India's success. With persistence in vision and strength of determination, the Government is a determinant factor in India's case of IT contrary to Porter's categorisation that Government is a non-determinant factor. Not only did the government envisioned, directed and promoted the industry, it also initially provided the market too in form of the government departments and the public sector companies. The publicly funded research in space, nuclear and defense provided the required boost to the Industry. The second non-determinant factor "Chance" does not seem to have favoured India in any manner. Be it Y2K problem, Dot Com boom or global spread of Internet, the opportunities were open to whole world. In fact, some of the chances that depended on infrastructure support such as Internet revolution were less favourable to India.

The intellectual capital is the biggest factor of India's success in IT. We discussed some other factors in section 7.1. As discussed previously, clustering is evident in our case. Clusters started with the concentration of qualified resources. One reason being the push from the local and central governments in form of sustained vision and incentives. Other reason is the availability of R&D and education industries which played an important role in mentoring the human capital.

Porter's Model mentions a Demand Condition at home front, but India's great leap in IT did not begin with great home demand. Even after several decades of India's success in IT, home demand portion is considerably small. Porter's model has the measurement scale in terms of GDP per capita as a measurement of the competitiveness. According to Porter (2002; p8), GDP is the best single, summary measure of microeconomic competitiveness available across all countries. The concept of per-capita GDP has several shortcomings. The parallel economy in India which may be the half of the GDP is not accounted. It also ignores the practice of bartering prevalent in rural India. It ignores voluntary and unpaid contributions as well as the local conditions. A dollar may not buy you a can of coke in the USA but may feed you for a week in India. Hence depending solely on any number does not show a fare picture even if the number is GDP. Second, the GDP reflects upon a nation and independent of the performance of any specific industries.

Porter's Diamond model fails on remaining two determinants (Related/Supporting Industries and Firm/Industry Structure/Strategy) also. The minimal presence of the hardware and other ancillary industries supports the weak dimension for the related and supporting industries. Similarly Rivalry and firm structure are also no determinant in Indian's case as their existence is not the primary causes of India's success. The infrastructure in India was anything but world class to prepare India for global competition. It is improving now to give a boost to Indian industry over the competitors but it was certainly not a determinant. Thus, it can be seen that Porter's diamond model is inadequate in this context and it fails in defining India's success in IT. Other studies too (Dayasindhu 2002 and Krishna et al. 2000:195) suggest that Porter's model does not explain the case of IT industry in India.

7.3. Software Export Success Model (SESM)

Since software export has been a major strength and a major portion of the Indian IT industry it is reasonable to review SESM here. Proposed by Heeks and Nicholson (2002), SESM has been applied to several software exporting nations (Nicholson and Sahay 2003). It was developed from the success factors of India, Ireland, and Israel, the original success cases. SESM consists of five major factors, some with important subcategories: demand (for software); national software vision and strategy; international linkages and trust; national software industry characteristics; and national software-related infrastructure. A number of common factors appear in these sources, for example, human capital factors, appear in all three sources; infrastructure appears in two of these sources but not in India. India emerged as the strongest nation among the three cases despite of faring poor in infrastructure. IT in general and software industry specifically does not need infrastructure the way traditional industries, say transportation or steel industries need. For long, the sceptics kept highlighting India's lower number of telephones, computers and internet users compared to other strong economies but ultimately none of these shortcomings could hinder the growth of Indian IT industry. On the contrary, the progress in IT sector helped India improve the infrastructure. The India advantages according to the SESM are shown in Table 15.

Table 15: The Software Export Success Model

Success Factors	India's Status
Demand	High external demand; weak domestic demand
National Vision & Strategy	Present; Climbing up the value chain
International Linkage and Trust	Reputation and trust through ISO/CMMI and law
Industry Characteristics	Competence, Clustering and Collaboration
Domestic Input/ Infrastructure	Human capital, R&D, Innovation, Cultural

Having an existing infrastructure based on an older and less efficient technology may actually prove as a stumbling block to the success. For example, in mobile phone technologies, the GSM helped the mobile phone industry to become an instant success in India while it is still struggling in the USA because of the existence of older but alternative CDMA/TDMA technologies. Similarly IBM's departure of 1970s allowed India to switch to the agile and open UNIX platform instead of the legacy systems. Thus, lack of infrastructure actually proved to be a blessing in disguise because it allowed the industry to get the best and most efficient technology as the starting point without having to deal with serious change management issues.

Trust is another highlight of this model where India's strong anti-piracy/copyright legislation for software and its adherence to the toughest international standards combined with the elements like freedom of press, democracy and diversity increased its trustworthiness in the eyes of prospective clients. Overall, barring infrastructure, this model defines India's success in software export pretty well.

7.4. Oval Model

The Oval Model of national software export success factors was proposed by Carmel (2003) as an improvement over the SESM. This model includes eight factors which are Government Vision and Policy, Human Capital, Quality of Life, Wages, The Industry, Capital, Technological Infrastructure, and Linkages (Carmel 2003). These factors are displayed in Figure 13.

Presence of contradictory factors such as wages and Quality of Life may be explained in this model by not insisting on presence of all of the eight factors. It also emphasizes on human capital. This model observes that the human capital takes one or two generations to develop. It removes some secondary factors of SESM, such as trust. The removal of the trust factor from the original SESM is not explained. Trust has played an important role in India's success. On legal side India builds trust through independent jury and strict laws such as Indian Copyright Act and the IT Act 2000. CMMI, ISO and other standards strengthen trust on standards front. The India brand further strengthens the trust. Wages may not be considered a factor our case as the wages are much lower in other sectors which did not show the kind of growth shown by the IT industry. Quality of Life is a new factor which was missing in SESM which is not applicable in our case. Capital is important for any industry. In fact, IT industry is not as capital intensive as many other industries such as steel. Role of infrastructure has been discussed in SESM section.

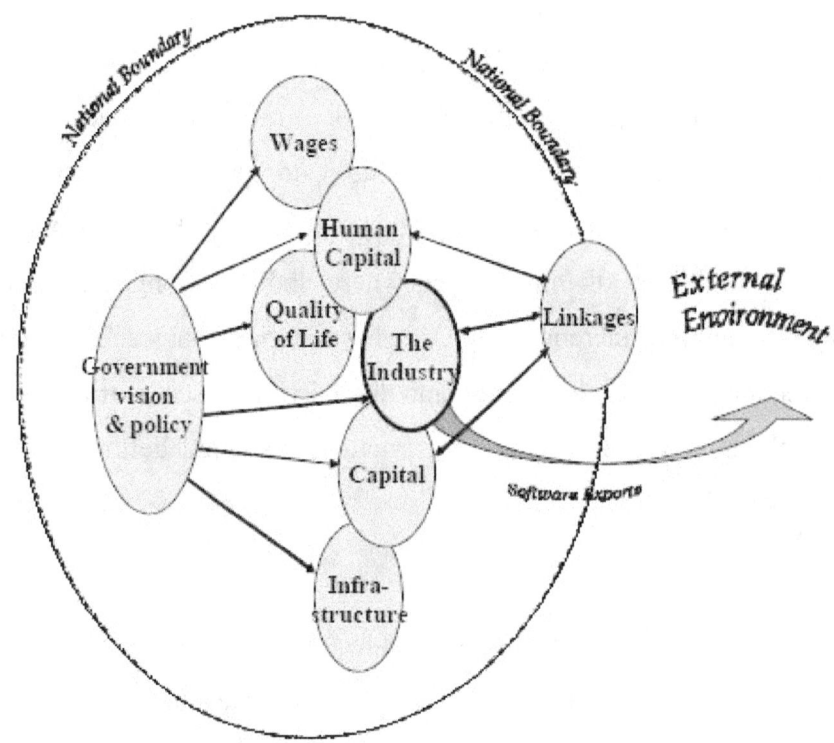

Figure 12: The Oval Model Depicting Eight Factors

This model suggests that Government can play a proactive or facilitating role in other seven factors. As we discussed in earlier sections, the role of the Government is undisputable in our case. Overall, the Oval model does not provide much value addition over SESM. In fact, the removal of the trust factor makes it less useful. The condition of presence on any number of factors out of total eight makes this model too general to be of any practical use in case of India or any other country.

7.5. Global Delivery Model

Globalization is sourcing capital from where it is cheapest, producing where it is most cost-effective and selling where it is most profitable without being constrained by national boundaries. Infosys used this concept to pioneer the Global Delivery Model (GDM) that leverages talent and infrastructure in different parts of the world to provide high-quality, rapid time-to-market solutions (Murthy 2003).

GDM takes advantage of the globalization of the economy. It capitalises on centres of technological excellence around the world and chose the best quality at the best price to create a winning combination from global resources. Under this model an American company may set up an R&D office in India, move manufacturing to China, and move its call centre in Brazil while running its US software office with Indian engineers.

This model is merely a smart business technique that aided the industry to meet the demands of clients effectively. It does not help in identifying the strengths or weaknesses of any country or cannot serve as a device to measure an industry's success. So, we cannot apply this model to our context.

7.6. Total Factor Productivity (TFP)

The Total Factor Productivity is often seen as the real driver of growth within an economy and studies reveal that whilst labour and investment are important contributors, TFP may account for up to as much as 60% of growth within economies.

The efficiency of an economy can be measured by TFP. In fact, TFP is now is considered the key indicator of competitiveness and is accepted as the main contributing factor of economic growth. The concept of TFP stresses that the technological sophistication and managerial innovativeness are the key factors for a sustained output growth as compared to capital investment.

Since Indian growth is not led by the FDI, the risk of bad loans is much less compared to the countries with only investment-led growth. TFP is backed by technology and efficiency growth. In China, FDI enterprises contribute most to TFP; local businesses are lagging. Unless national enterprises are privatized further and institutional funds used more efficiently, TFP-led growth will slacken in China (Majumder 2006). In contrast, private enterprise is flourishing in India and a large contributor to TFP.

7.7. China Model

China model is based on better infrastructure, cheap labour, and large capital investments including FDI. It has little provision for innovation and technology. It also lacks proper representation from the domestic private enterprise. The first private airline in China was allowed to fly in 2005. China's FDI is ten times more than India's though it ranks lower than India[94] in terms of GCI. More than 60 per cent of the FDI China receives is from its diaspora. These investments are capital-intensive with hardly any technology component.

China, despite soaking up FDI, trails in ushering in innovative technology, even in industries where it dominates. Huang and Khanna (2003) remind that India is increasingly building from the ground up while China is pursuing a top-down approach. They make a distinction between the two economies, and state that the Chinese model is not a strong platform for sustainable development.

Over 90 per cent of China's infrastructure development has been through government funding, leaving little for harmonious socialistic growth. Even after reforms, the slow speed of privatization of national enterprises has prevented them from adopting modern technology resulting in a big gulf between home-grown and FDI-backed industries. China's weak legal structure, inadequate Intellectual Property Rights system and the not-so-transparent banking organization are areas of concern for foreign investors (Majumder 2006).

China model may be successful for countries working for a lead in manufacturing sectors. But it falls short in case of Knowledge sector. An examination of China model makes it clear that the factors of the success of the Indian IT industry are completely different. The basic China model ingredients such as FDI, lack of domestic private enterprise, government's complete control on banking system played no role in the success of the Indian IT industry. China model also lacks the basic intangible ingredients of the Indian IT industry: innovation, intellectual capital, diversity and free flow of thoughts. Indian IT industry has some cultural advantages too which may not be explained in China model.

---

[94]According to the Global Competitiveness Index, 2006 of the World Economic Forum, China was ranked 54 and India 43 in the ascending order among 121 countries.

7.8. Gradualism Growth Model

Gradualism Growth model provides a broad policy vision without rigid guidelines for change management. According to Ahya et al. (2004), India's approach is gradual and consensual. In that sense, India has been a unique emerging market model, which has put greater emphasis on evolving a well developed institutional framework including autonomous judiciary, a democratic political set-up and redistribution agencies.

India's internal and external reforms, including deregulation of business investments, deregulation of factor input and output prices, significant reductions in tax rates and relaxation of restrictions on foreign capital investment may not be reflecting in GDP growth but they have improved macro stability and reduced volatility in output. The GDP growth trend in India does not reflect its full potential as the growth is steady but slow. India will achieve its potential growth of 7% plus over the next 10 years if it addresses its large government revenue deficit (tax and non-tax revenues less revenue expenditure) and its need for infrastructure development (Ahya et al. 2004).

This model defines the nature of India's slow and steady growth but it does not explain the causes. Hence, this model does not help identifying the success factors behind India's success in IT.

7.9. Critical Success Factors

Chandra (2006) provides a long list of the Key Factors to explain the Success of India's IT industry:

- Human capital
- Early-mover advantage
- Low investment requirements in software industry
- Early investments in engineering education and privatization of education created a large talent pool
- Body shopping exposed a large population to new ways of working.
- Professionally trained entrepreneurs

- Vigorous efforts at assimilating new technology and good management practices

- Competitive costs, high quality and delivery performance

- Selective support to industry in an otherwise constraining environment by a few enlightened bureaucrats and the role of NASSCOM in influencing policy

- Lack of effective implementation of restrictive policies allowed market forces a significant play in the early phase. The economy was liberalized in later years

- Highly entrepreneurial IT training and private education industry which responds quickly to fill skill gaps and opportunities

- Positive government policies and lack of regulation meant few barriers

- Large population created competition for engineering seats and jobs

- Competition from MNCs came when indigenous firms were prepared

Most of these factors are in conformance to the views expressed in chapter 5 and have played a role in India's success except privatization of education. The privatization of education is not true in context of Indian IT as the most successful entrepreneurs, managers and engineers came from the institutions like IITs and the universities which are autonomous but either run by the government or at least funded and subsidized by the government. Besides, the Indian government made every effort to support the industry by providing right atmosphere. On the contrary, the boost in private sector education in IT, computer science and related engineering branches is a direct result of the success of the IT industry.

7.10. Indian Information Technology Success (IITS) Model

Sections 7.1 to 7.8 discussed various models from the Indian IT success perspective. No single model could best describe India's ever-growing success in the IT sector. There are considerable overlaps and contradictions in existing models as seen in previous sections. Furthermore, the categorization of success factors in these models did not always apply to the IT industry in India and where they did apply they had very little explanatory power. A close scrutiny of the existing models combined with our own research findings (see previous chapters) of the Indian IT industry's success led us to build a more robust model that can be applied to different clusters/regions, to different cultures/nations, to large and small, private and public sector industries. The model shall be called as Indian Information Technology Success (IITS) model.

It is important to highlight the differences IITS has with other existing models. Be it Porter's, SESM or Oval, existing models insist on availability of infrastructure as a pre-requisite to development. The reality has a slight twist here. Dependence on infrastructure changes with other conditions. One standard global benchmark cannot be applied for infrastructure. This is especially true in case of IT. For example, a development model that binds success of Internet in any country to tele-density is a little imbalanced. Considering infrastructure as a prerequisite to success is one reason of several models' failure in explaining India's success. Dependence on infrastructure reduces as the technology matures. This dependence falls much sharply in case of IT and related industries. The relationship between the maturity of the industry and the infrastructure is shown in Figure 14 (adopted from Sharma 2006).

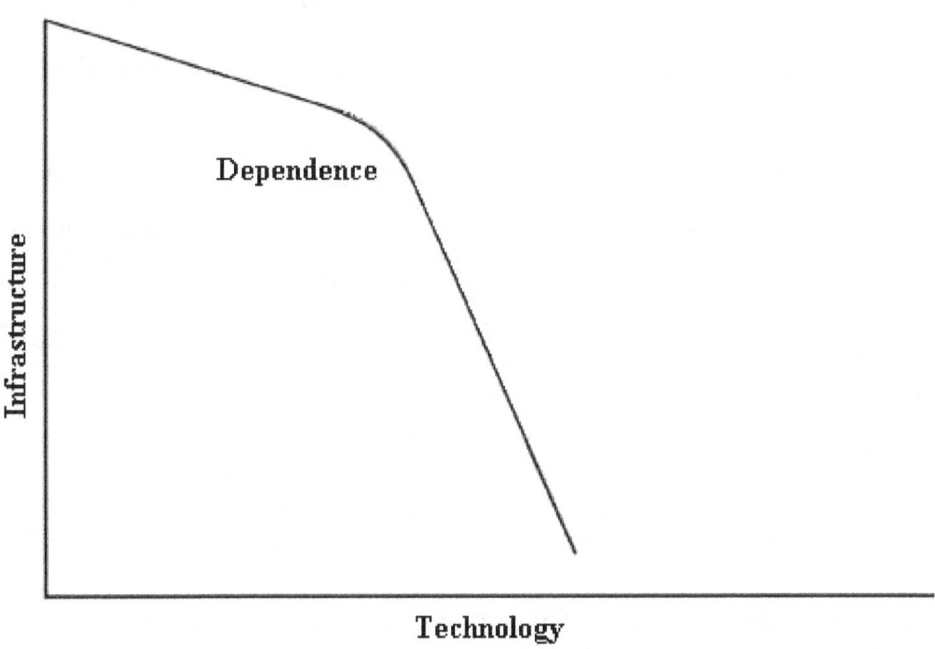

Figure 13: Maturity of the Industry and the Dependence on Infrastructure

Nagala (2005) suggests that the activities of the IT related government agencies, STPIs and the global Indian diaspora are the three factors that helped India's success in IT. There is no

89

doubt that the first two have played an important role in this success but the same cannot be said about the diaspora issue. Besides Sam Pitroda, no other non-resident Indian made a remarkable difference. In fact American companies like Microsoft, IBM, Oracle, and Intel have done more work in India than the companies owned or headed by the people of Indian origin living abroad. Unlike China's FDI driven model, Indian diaspora, though helped a lot in growth of IT Industry in USA, it was not instrumental in India's success in IT.

Like infrastructure and global diaspora, there are other elements which did not matter much in case of India's success. The IITS ignores these factors and groups them together as Minimal Factors. Capital is another component worth mention. It is included in some models as a factor for success. Capital is required across the companies and the nations as contrary to an ingredient for success for a specific industry or country. Also, the success of an industry in a country is not directly related to the amount or availability of capital at any stage. For these reasons, IITS considers capital too as a Minimal Factor. Elements such as home demand, low cost, chance, familiarity with English, Infrastructure in traditional sense, such as roads, telephone landlines and short term opportunistic plans considered to be success factors in the existing models are also seen as minimal factors for IITS.

The next step is to identify the major components of the IITS model by taking clues from India's case in IT. Chapter 5 described the success factors in detail which form the basis to carve out the model. The critical success factors can be classified semantically into five factors: Core, Leadership, Market, Stabilization, and Growth. The elements covered in each of the factors are listed below (self-explanatory and not exhaustive):

Core Factors

- Human Resources
- Cultural strength
- Tradition of arts, sciences, knowledge, and education
- Ethnic and linguistic diversity
- Democracy, Freedom of thought, profession, language, practices

Leadership Factors

- Strategy, Leadership, Direction,

- Incentives, Vision and government policy

- Law and Judiciary

- Established Financial System

- Excellent management practices and adherence to world standards

1. Market Factors
   - Readiness of the market, Demand

   - Competitiveness

   - Shift or advancement in technology such as satellite links

   - Global thinking as contrary to protectionism

   - Reliability

   - Economy, Efficiency and Lower Overall Cost

   - Learning Organizations

   - Supremacy of the customer

   - Implementing Standards and Quality Controls

2. Stabilization Factors
   - Climbing up the value chain

   - Innovation

   - R&D

   - Acting Global

3. Growth Factors
   - Building Goodwill, brand name

   - Reliability – includes independent, impartial and effective judiciary,

   - Collaborations, Alliances and Partnerships

On the basis of the above analysis, the IITS can now be given a more meaningful pattern thereby giving shape to our new model. We call the new model as "The Pyramid Model of Indian IT Success" depicted in Figure 14.

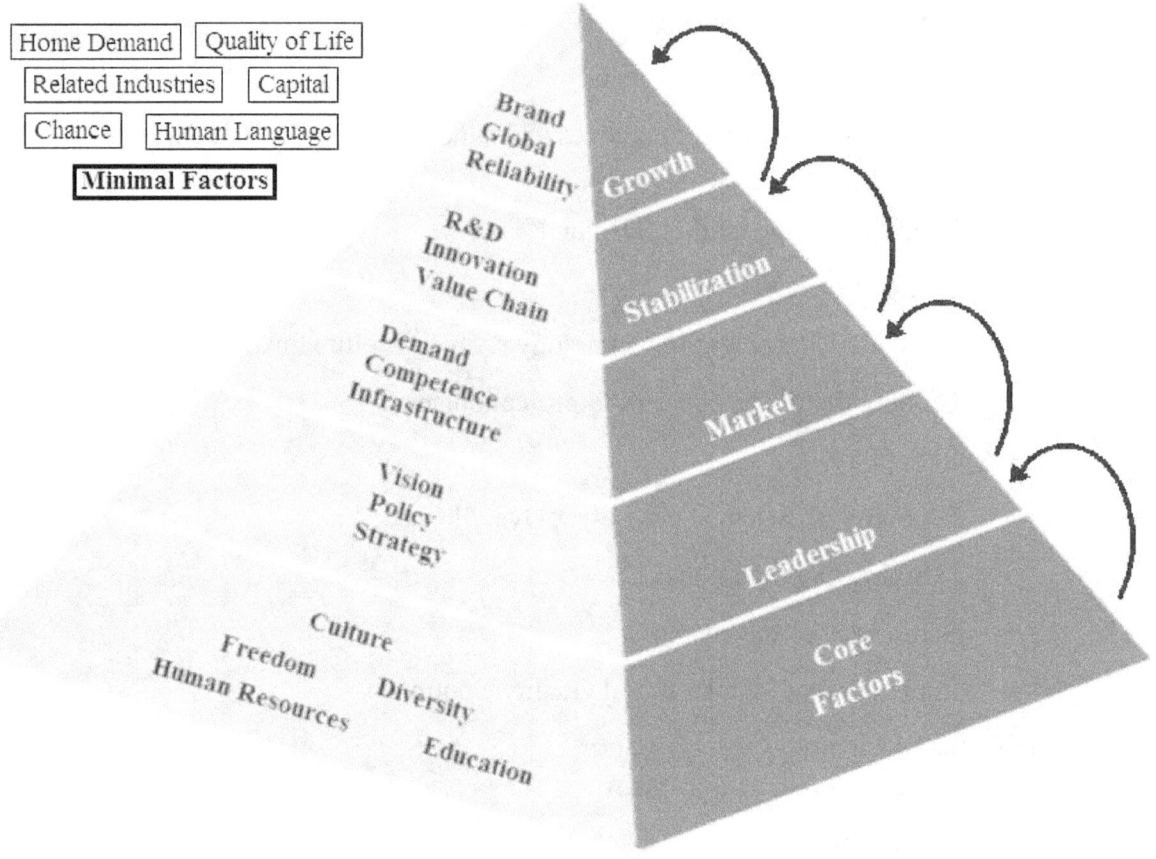

Figure 14: Indian Information Technology Success (IITS) Model

The IITS model indicates that the success of an IT industry is multi-layered and can be represented by five major factors represented by five layers. They are: Core, Leadership, Market, Stabilization, and Growth. The layers are stacked from bottom to top in a specific order in the form of a pyramid. Each layer has its own critical success elements. The Core Factors layer is the minimum requirement for this model. After achieving competence in one layer, a move to the next layer is made. This move is required to sustain the success in the long run until reaching the top. These five layers are not independent of each other. They are connected sequentially. In other words, an industry cannot ignore a layer in order to reach the top of the pyramid (success).

There is a sixth group outside the pyramid, called Minimal factors. As the name implies, these factors are literally minimal or even neutral in some cases. This layer includes elements that are either not specific to IT industry or are not required at all. It includes vague factors that cannot be tested as a cause of the success such as chance. It also includes factors that are universally required across industries and nations such as capital. It also includes factors that may influence the success in the short term in a specific case but cannot be applied as a required condition for the success itself or its sustainability, such as home demand, related industries or the familiarity with a specific language.

7.11. Emulating the Success - By Other Industries

The success of the Indian IT industry has influenced other sectors of the Indian economy. The growth in other areas can be accelerated with the help of advancements in IT. For example the drug trials or designing a geo-stationary satellite take much less time with help of appropriate IT solutions. Today, Indian business, government, and consumers have access to a multitude of new software and hardware products to make their work more efficient and their personal life more enjoyable.

Emulating the IT success is much easier in the knowledge industry and other advanced technologies as the components at the various layers are same. Let us test cereal production, nuclear research, and satellite development on IITS. Core Factors such as human resources, education etc., are available in plenty. The next step is to see if the leadership factors are present. India has envisioned and provided required policies and strategies for growth. India has a reasonable demand, competence and infrastructure for the next (market) layer. To gain stability in these areas, the elements of R&D, Innovation and Value Chain are required. These elements have been provided by the public sector and the autonomous research institutes (in case of Agro sector). Recent Indo-US Nuclear Co-operation Treaty is the proof of Indian Nuclear Technology sector's success at the Growth Layer with all three components of Brand, Reliability and Global. The deals with European Union (EU) on satellite design and launch show that the Satellite industry has arrived at the Growth Layer. Similarly, India's ability to come forward to help the Asian countries after Tsunami of December 2004 and to the USA after hurricane Katrina puts India's agriculture sector at Growth Layer[95].

For other industries, there is a lot to learn from Indian IT sector. It has organizations that are being creative in addressing the professional development of the employees. The adherence of the Indian IT industry to the quality and standards is a sure thing to be adopted by the industries looking for success. Strong work ethics too can help any industry to excel. IT succeeded because the required human resources were available in plenty. This fact indicates that local availability of raw material may help industries excel. IT firms have set new standards in accounting and corporate governance too. The high standards of management practiced in Indian IT firms and the tremendous employment opportunities offered by the industry have had significant effects on the confidence, aspirations, and work ethic of young professionals in India. The leading software firms have pioneered a movement to modernize Indian management practices,

Taking lessons from IT's path of adopting and implementing standards and controls, other industries are also seriously looking at CMMI. Embedded Systems & Software (EmSyS), a unit of the Electrical & Electronics Division of L&T, has become the first systems company to be assessed for using all the components of CMMI's Level 5 model. And as CMMI matures, more product and system companies are expected to follow suit during the latter half of 2003.

Other industries are closely watching the role of acquisitions as a tool of swift growth of the IT industry. The Tata group's acquisition of Korea based Daewoo Trucks, and UK based Tetley and Good Earth is a good example of this route. Table 16 shows some examples of the recent bids and acquisitions by non-IT Indian companies. The IITS model suits knowledge intensive industries which require highly skilled and innovative human resource with capability of abstract thinking and decision making.

---

[95]It shows India's transition from a net importer of food grains into a country having enough surpluses to supply globally in case of need.

Table 16: Some Recent Acquisitions by Indian Firms in UK

Indian Company	Company Being Acquired	Cost	Year
Tata Group	Corus (Ex. British Steel)	4.3 billion pounds	Pending
Tata Group	Tetley Tea	270 million pounds	2000
Tata Group	Tyco Global Network	69 million pounds	2004
Apeejay International	Typhoo (Premier Foods)	80 million pounds	2005
United Breweries	Whyte & Mackay	400 million pounds	Pending

Biotechnology is one such area. Like the IT, it is knowledge-intensive and requires great skills and adherence to strict scientific methodologies. This sector provides a new opportunity to tap into areas such as drug discovery, clinical trials and bio-informatics to India's low-cost, but highly efficient, work force. The expertise of the Indian doctors, managers, programmers and administrators is already being utilized by India. With 25% growth rate[96], Biotechnology is fast becoming a high growth area for India. Experts suggests that India's entry into a global patent regime under the World Trade Organization will help further boost investments by Western companies in biotechnology.

7.12. Emulating the Success - By Other Countries

Not all developing countries can follow India's path. However, they can reap the software rewards of hi-tech jobs, capabilities and income if they learn to combine successful tactics, strategy and vision ~ Heeks (1999).

This section explores if the IITS model can be adopted successfully by other countries. The first choice is China with Philippines being the other country. In the end, it also tests the IITS model on US too which is the undisputed king of the software industry.

China already has a software industry that serves mainly to domestic market and probably uses Chinese as the language of communication. It has a millennia long tradition of emulating

---

[96]AFAR (URL: http://www.asianresearch.org/articles/2222.html)

and improvising Indian models[97]. It is also trying hard to adopt India's success in IT. Will they succeed in their mission? According to IITS model, China should overcome the two significant obstacles that might hinder IT growth:

IITS prescribes freedom as a core factor for the success. The element of freedom incorporates freedom of thoughts and information exchange as well as freedom of private enterprise. Being a communist country, China does not provide the socio-political environment promoting the idea of free mind. Since the Core Factors are the minimum requirements for success according to the IITS, China needs to take necessary steps towards improvising the environment if it wants to emulate India's success in IT.

Another factor to be examined is the Human Language element from the Minimal Factors of the IITS model in Chinese context. English is currently the language of the IT. Recently China is stressing the needs on English education which is a good move but unfortunately the benefits of the efforts may not be reaped instantly. China is already facing the negative growth due to the one-child policy. By the time this new education system starts producing results there will be a comparatively small young population of working age to support a much larger senior population. The best option for China is not to try emulating Indian model and continue with their existing growth model so that the resources earned today may be utilized later to address a much serious problem of supporting the greying population.

Philippines is another country that has a large diaspora in the USA besides familiarity to US English and a budding BPO industry. Let us see if Philippines can emulate India's success with a stronger focus on IT-enabled services. American English is taught in Philippines. It follows a democratic system. The freedom element of Core Factors as a requirement for fostering flexibility and creativity is available. It has comparatively lower costs of operation. Labor costs are higher than in India (Jatras 2001) and overall cost may be much higher. More

---

[97]Martial arts were passed to Chinese by the Indian Buddhist monks. China improvised those and later exported in such a way that most of us get surprised when we read that India is the original birth place of martial arts. Same is true about their knowledge of iron around 500 B.C. The concept of a merciful God was adopted by the Chinese in form of Buddhist philosophy that came from India through monks and the traders. Many methods, such as the building of pagodas, the making of statues, and the practice of fresco etc., were learned by the Chinese scholars who studied in India.

or less, it has other elements of the Core Factors too. It has good infrastructure built by the US bases but political instability, corruption and absence of strong legal structure make the country less reliable for IT exports. There is not much of a domestic market. Philippines can easily stay at the Market Factors stage. It has fair chances to get a reasonable share of growing BPO market. It needs to increase its reliability to climb higher in value-chain.

The scope of most of the models defining India's success is limited to the developing countries. The IITS model has no such limitation. That is why the third country we are testing is the USA. India and USA have a lot in common. They both are free, diverse, culturally rich democratic countries. The both respect education and have a huge number of top class educational institutions. They both have a large number of highly qualified human resources. It is obvious that USA has all the Core Factors. There seems to be some lopsided vision in form of recent laws passed to stop outsourcing by some states. But overall, USA has excellent vision, policy and strategy, the elements of the Leadership Factors. It has the demand, competence and infrastructure of the Market Factors. We should remember that the extraordinary strengths of the USA in the Core Factors of freedom (of enterprise and ideas), education and diversity help it at the Market Layer to be able to maintain competence. H1B visa is one such example where USA can easily fill the gap of the human resources with help of the above strengths of Core Layer. In context of IT, the American enterprise is already ahead of the world in R&D, Innovation and ascending in value chain. Thus, US IT industry has already arrived at the Stabilization Layer. What about the last layer? In IT also the Brand America is known to the world. American enterprise is reliable and has a global presence. Hence, the United States is an undisputed success case in IT according to the IITS model.

8. DISCUSSIONS AND CONCLUSIONS

8.1. Discussions

This book explored the success of IT sector in India. There is no doubt that India excelled in this domain. The statistics show that the Indian IT industry has grown rapidly in the last few decades. India has the right mixture of the ingredients for success. It is making proper use of its resources. The success is sustainable too. The IITS model found many components at various factor layers which created the initial success. The vision of leaders and the policies by the government including STPI, Incentives, liberalisation and deregulation promoted the industry. The strong vision of Indian leaders along with the rich industrial culture led to the creation of the MCIT, NASSCOM and IBEF thereby enabling the coordination of various agencies that deal with the information technology. The implementation of software technology parks is another big achievement where business, government, and academia can come together both for networking and production.

With human resources being the most important ingredient of IITS model, success is sustainable for Indian IT industry. The language of the industry may shift from English to Chinese or any other language but the extra-ordinary exposure of Indians to linguistic diversity will keep them ahead of others in learning, adopting and effectively using the new language of business. The growth of IT is not mutually exclusive of other advanced technologies; hence, there is a harmonious growth of more knowledge based technologies in India.

While testing existing theories in explaining India's success, it was found that there is unjustified stress on low wages in India. It is the low overall cost combined with best management practices that really made the difference of economy. Some scholars insisted that it was the English language that played an important role in India's IT success but they fail to see that India's IT brand is seen equally effective in non-English speaking countries such as Germany, China and Japan.

Unique qualities of Indian culture such as diversity, democracy and respect for education also came up as hidden but very important ingredients of this success. To sustain the success, India will have to become more proactive in the industry and develop a lead in research, invention and innovation instead of acing reactive as currently developing and supporting the innovation of others.

Indian diaspora is heavily represented in research, medicine, education, accounting, business, science and engineering. India has started taking initiative to provide right environment to its largely successful diaspora to return or at least participate and reap benefits from India's recent success in IT.

The advantage of the IT revolution should carry the spirit of Sanskrit phrase *Bahujan Hitaya Bahujan Sukhaya*[98] and ensure that a larger number of people and industries are benefited by the confidence regained by the IT. The major sectors which are witnessing a special thrust for adoption and implementation of IT are government organizations, Insurance, Banks, Aviation, Energy, Financial Institutions, Defense, Ports, Customs, Telecommunications, Biotechnology, Education and Research Institutes. Health care organizations, particularly those in private sector have started adopting IT in their functioning. The Indian government encourages other sectors too to benefit from this ever-growing technology in order to enhance their growth. Competitiveness and efficiency of the Indian IT companies came up as strength in this area which helped them shine before the competition.

Another important consideration is whether lessons we can learn from India's success can be applied to other developing countries. Interested countries should explore the factors that made Indian IT companies highly competitive and efficient in the market and try to adopt the same. Language policies that include English as a medium of instruction at secondary and higher education could serve as a starting point for developing nations interested in becoming IT-competent nation. In addition to this, good management strategies and practices, work culture and ethics and improvement of the infra-structure to suit the dynamic industrial era of the globe should be adopted as well. If necessary, business entrepreneurs and government bureaucrats could take help from their Indian counterparts in order to emulate this success efficiently and effectively.

---

[98] An old Sanskrit phrase that literally means: Welfare and happiness for a larger number of people.

Furthermore, an interesting future area of research into this subject could be to see if this growth can help India eradicate its social problems such as poverty and poor healthcare, and elevate its status from a developing nation to a developed nation. This should be possible if the government policies not only encourage IT penetration in all sectors of industries, large or small but also ensure that the economic growth from IT benefits the lower socio-economic groups as well. If such growth and plans are found to have positive effects, other developing countries would be attracted to emulate them within the contexts of their own national goals.

8.2. Conclusions

India is fast becoming one of the world's software superpowers, proving that in a globalized world, developing nations not only can succeed, developing nations can lead. ~ Bill Clinton[99], Ex President, USA (Hyderabad, April 2000)

This book analysed some existing models on the success of IT in India while assessing the strengths and weaknesses of Indian IT industry. It reviewed key indicators and facts to ensure that India's success is not just hype. The challenges India had to face throughout the process in order to succeed in its IT industry were discussed at length. It describes the major Success Factors that played a vital role in the success. It not only presents these factors in a systematic way but also highlights the most important ones that need to be paid special attention to. A new model, Indian Information Technology Success (IITS) model was developed. Model validation is also important. One possible direction in future is to validate and thus enhance the model by conducting case studies of IT development/success in developing nations.

It is clear that India's success in IT is no accident but a combination of cultural strengths, government policies and free enterprise besides hard work. India's mature and robust education system had been providing the human resources the western world before working for India in to IT and other advanced areas at the right time. India's IT industry displays the inner strength of free and innovative Indian enterprise. It is not driven by FDI but built ground up to be long lasting.

---

[99]Rediff Special (URL: http://www.rediff.com/us/2000/apr/08us3.htm)

This book explored the possibility of applying India's IT experience on other industries. The resource-based theory of the firm suggests that the firms must develop valuable, rare, and costly to copy firm-specific capabilities to gain a sustained competitive advantage (Wernerfelt 1984). IITS model suggests that most of the ingredients of this success are valuable and available to other industries in India. In fact, the book specifies that the IT success is already being emulated successfully by other industrial sectors especially high-technology ones in India. Though, applying the success to other countries is not as easy since there are several cultural components that may not be created instantly or imported[100] like other tangible ingredients. The research tested that this success may not be imitated by China and Philippines due to lack of certain basic ingredients say freedom, private entrepreneurship in case of China and absolute number of qualified human resources in case of Philippines.

The Indian IT industry is growing fast in comparison to other industries. It is also growing when compared with other countries by successfully overcoming the challenges. The Indian IT industry has moved up the value chain. Though the growth rate could be faster, the growth will continue at least at the same pace in the next ten to twenty years. Indian economy is getting stronger and IT industry is making its presence felt globally. The demand for software services is also growing consistently. India may get tough competition from China in future but currently it is consolidating its competitive position through overseas M&As. Other developing country locations may become active and Indian companies have started outsourcing the lower-end jobs due to lower cost compared to India.

Besides combating the internal challenges such as illiteracy, Indian IT industry needs to continue getting more sophisticated and innovative to retain its position as a global leader. This would require better infrastructure and spread of the industry beyond current clusters so that the hitherto untapped potential of lower cost locations within the country can be utilized. The domestic market also needs to grow beyond the public sector and the government departments to provide a stimulus to the development of a larger and stronger IT industry in India which is less prone to external factors.

---

[100]H1B visas in USA are good example of importing these cultural ingredients.

REFERENCES[101]

Ahya, Chetan et al. (2004). India and China: A Special Economic Analysis. Morgan Stanley.

Ashraf, Tariq. (2004). Information technology and public policy: a socio human profile of Indian digital revolution. The International Information & Library Review (2004) 36, 309–318

Athreye, Suma S. (2005). The Indian software industry and its evolving service capability. Industrial and Corporate Change, Vol. 14, pp 393-418.

Balasubramanyam, V.N. and Balasubramanyam, A. (1997) International trade in services: the case of India's computer software, World Economy, 20(6), 829-843.

Bagchi, Subroto. (2005). Lessons in Entrepreneurship from the Indian IT Industry. MindTree Consulting (P) Ltd. [online] http://www.mindtree.com/docs/Entrepreneurship-Indian-IT-Industry.pdf.

Bajpai, Nirupam and Shastri, Vanita. (1998). Software Industry in India: A Case Study. Development Discussion Paper No. 667 December 1998. Harvard Institute for International Development.

Bajwa, G.S. (2003). ICT policy in India in the era of liberalization: Its impact and consequences. Global Built Environment Review 3, 49–61.

Birdsall, Nancy. (2002). Brain Drain and Human Development Report 2001. United Nations Development Program [online] http://www.undp.org.lb/tokten/braindrain.html

Business World. (2004). Most Respected Company Awards 2004. [online] http://www.businessworld.in/nov1504/sector_winners2.asp. Retrieved on 2006-10-10.

Business Week. (2006). Major Players in Outsourcing. Special Report -Outsourcing/Online Extra. Business Week January 30, 2006. [online] http://www.businessweek.com/magazine/content/06_05/b3969412.htm

Business Week. (1999). N.R. Narayana Murthy, Founder, Infosys Technologies, India (int'l edition). Business Week June 14, 1999. [online] http://www.businessweek.com/1999/99_24/b3633065.htm.

Butler, William. (1885). From Boston to Bareilly and Back, Phillip & Hunt, New York.

---

[101]All the URLs listed in the references section were last accessed on January 16, 2007 to ensure availability.

Carmel, Erran. (2003). The New Software Exporting Nations: Success Factors. The Electronic Journal on Information Systems in Developing Countries.

Chakravorty Bhaswati. (2006). Intellectual Property: Gathering Steam. Dataquest (July 25, 2006). [online] http://www.dqindia.com/content/DQTop20_2006/giants06/2006/106072528.asp.

Chandra, Vandana. (2006). Technology, Adaptation, and Exports - How some developing Countries got it right. World Bank,Washington DC.

Das, Gurcharan. (2002). India Unbound: From Independence to the Global Information Age. Penguin Books India, New Delhi.

Das, Sudhanshu R. (2006). Cash in on the skills, cast away the divide. Hindu Business Line, July 19, 2006. [online] http://www.thehindubusinessline.com/2006/07/19/stories/2006071900351100.htm

Dataquest. (1998). The DQ top 20 (July 15, 1998.).

Dayasindhu, N. (2002). Embeddedness, knowledge transfer, industry clusters and global competitiveness: a case study of the Indian software industry, Technovation, 22, 551560.

Desai, Lord Meghnad. (2000). Commanding Heights. Interview conducted December 07, 2000 [online] http://www.pbs.org/wgbh/commandingheights/lo/resources/pdf_index.html#int_meghnaddesai

Elliott, Michael. (2006). India Inc. - Why the World's Biggest Democracy is the Next Great Economic Superpower and what it means for America, Time (June 26, 2006).

Evans, Peter. (1995). Embedded Autonomy. States and Industrial Transformation. Princeton, N.J. Princeton University Press.

Friedman, Thomas L. (2005). The World Is Flat: A Brief History of the Twenty-first Century. Farrar, Straus and Giroux, New York.

Gibson, Stan. (2005). Outsourcing & Services, eWeek August 1, 2005.

Gordon, Raymond G., Jr. (ed.) (2005). Ethnologue: Languages of the World, Fifteenth edition. Dallas, Tex.: SIL International. [online] http://www.ethnologue.com/.

Heeks, Richard. (2006). Analysing the Software Sector in Developing Countries Using Competitive Advantage Theory. Paper No. 25. The Development Informatics working paper series. Institute for Development Policy and Management, University of Manche ster, UK.

Heeks, Richard. (1999). Software Strategies in Developing Countries. Paper No. 6. The Development Informatics working paper series. Institute for Development Policy and Management, University of Manche ster, UK.

Heeks, Richard. (1996). India's Software Industry: State Policy, Liberalization and Industrial Development, Sage Publications, New Delhi, Thousand Oaks, London.

Heeks, Richard and Nicholson, Brian. (2002). Software Export Success Factors and Strategies in Developing and Transitional Economies, Proceedings IFIP Working Group 9.4 Conference, IIMB Bangalore, India, 29-31 May 2002.

Hofstadter, Douglas R. (1979). Goedel, Escher, Bach: an Eternal Golden Braid, NY: Basic Books.

Horowitz, Shel. (2003). Principled Profit: Marketing That Puts People First. AWM Books, Northampton MA.

HRD. (2006). Annual report of the Ministry of Human Resources Development. Government of India 2005-06.

Huang, Yeshang and Khanna, Tarun. (2003). Can India Overtake China? Foreign Policy – July | August 2003.

IBEF-KPMG. (2006). Information Technology – India Everywhere at World Wconomic Federation Davos 2006. [online] http://www.ibef.org/download/IT_sectoral.pdf. Last Modification Date: November 21, 2006.

Jatras, T. (2001). Can India retain its reign as outsourcing king? Forbes.com, February 28, 2001.

Kapur, Devesh. (2002). The Causes and Consequences of India's IT Boom. India Review 1(2), April 2002, 91-110.

Kearney. (2005). Kearney Offshore Location Attractiveness Study of 2005 [online] http://www.atkearney.com/main.taf?p=1,5,1,168

Kremer, M. et al. (2005). Teacher Absence in India: A Snapshot, Journal of the European Economic Association 3 (2-3): 658-667.

Krishna, S., Ojha, A.K. and Barrett, M. (2000). Competitive advantage in the software industry: an analysis of the Indian experience. Information Technology in Context, C. Avgerou & G. Walsham (eds), Ashgate, Aldershot, UK, 182197.

Krishnan, R.T. and G.N. Prabhu. (1999). Innovation in the Indian Information Technology Industry: A Study of the Software Product Development Process. Science Technology & Society, Vol. 7, No. 1, 91-115 (2002) DOI: 10.1177/097172180200700105 © 2002 SAGE Publications.

Lakha, Salim. (1994). The New International Division of Labor and the Indian Computer Software Industry. Modern Asian Studies, Vol. 28 pp 381-408.

Landes, David S. (2002). "The South American Way" and "Celestial Empire: Stasis and Retreat." The Wealth and Poverty of Nations 1998: 311-349. Rpt. in Readings for Issues in Global Competition. Ed. Professor James B. Burnham. Fall 2002.

Lema, R. and Hesbjerg, B. (2003). The Virtual Extension: A Search for Collective Efficiency in the Software Cluster in Bangalore, Roskilde University, Denmark.

Libicki, M. (2005). From Intimacy, Vulnerability. Conquest in Cyberspace. (To appear).

Majumder, S. (2006). FDI: Will India edge out China? Business Line ePaper, Friday, Oct 27, 2006 [online]
http://www.thehindubusinessline.com/2006/10/27/stories/2006102700080800.htm

Manohar, B. Murali. (2005). Information Development, Sage Publications. Vol 21, No. 1.

Mathur, V. K. (1999). Human Capital-Based Strategy for Regional Economic Development. Economic Development Quarterly, 13/3: 203-216

Mulhearn, J. (2000). Evolution and Globalization of the Indian Information Technology Industry: Protected Insular State Enterprises to Private Global Software Exporters.

Murthy, Narayana N. R. (2003). India's experience in developing a vibrant software industry - Lessons for Thailand. Speech Delivered at the Thailand Science Park, June 22, 2003.

Murthy, Narayana N. R. (2001). Commanding Heights. Interview conducted February 5, 2001 [online]
http://www.pbs.org/wgbh/commandingheights/lo/resources/pdf_index.html#prof_narayanamurthy.pdf.

Nagala, Sarala V. (2005). India's Story of Success: Promoting the Information Technology Industry. Stanford Journal of International Relations, 6(1) [online]
http://www.stanford.edu/group/sjir/6.1.toc.html.

Nandy, Pritish. (1998). This Bane of Swadeshi Politics. Rediff On The Net. March 30, 1998 issue at http://www.rediff.com/news/1998/mar/30nandy.htm.

NASSCOM. (2006a). Knowledge Professionals Fact Sheet 2006 [online] http://www.nasscom.in/Nasscom/templates/NormalPage.aspx?id=6314.

NASSCOM. (2006b). Survey 2006. Press Release Note [online] http://www.nasscom.in/Nasscom/templates/NormalPage.aspx?id=28833.

NASSCOM. (2006c). Strategic Review 2006: The IT Industry in India [online] http://www.nasscom.in/Nasscom/templates/NormalPage.aspx?id=2538.

NASSCOM. (2005a). Strategic Review 2005:The IT Industry in India [online] http://www.nasscom.in/Nasscom/templates/LandingPage.aspx?id=28670.

NASSCOM. (2005b). NASSCOM-Hewitt Total Rewards Study 2004 [online] http://www.nasscom.in/Nasscom/templates/NormalPage.aspx?id=4960.

Nilles, Jack M. (1999). Electronic Commerce and New Ways of Working in India. Jala International Inc. Los Angeles and Bonn [online] http://www.ecatt.com/country/india/inhalt_in.htm.

Nicholson. B. and Sahay, S. (2003). Building Iran's software industry: Assessment of Plans and Prospects, Electronic Journal of IS in Developing Countries, 13 [online] http://www.is.cityu.edu.hk/research/ejisdc/vol13.htm.

Parthasarathi , Ashok. (2003). Nature 422, 17-18 (6 March 2003) | doi:10.1038/422017a [online] http://www.nature.com/nature/journal/v422/n6927/full/422017a.html#a1.

Planning Commission: Tenth Five Year Plan 2002-2007. Chapter 7.4 Information Technology. p 809 [online] http://planningcommission.nic.in/plans/planrel/fiveyr/10th/volume2/v2_ch7_4.pdf.

Porter, M. E. (1998). The Competitive Advantage of Nations, New York: The Free Press.

Prahalad and Hamel. (1990). The core competence of the corporation. Harvard Business Review, 68(3), 79-93.

Ramesh, Jairam. (2001). Commanding Heights Interview conducted July 01, 2001 [online] http://www.pbs.org/wgbh/commandingheights/lo/resources/pdf_index.html#int_jairamramesh.

Rediff. (2005). India's top 15 BPO firms. Rediff Business (June 8, 2005) [online] http://www.rediff.com/money/2005/jun/08bpo2.htm.

Rudolph, Matthew C. J. (May 2000). Losing the IT advantage? Business Standard. [online] http://www.people.cornell.edu/pages/mcr4/Business%20Standard%20__MCJR%2007-05-2000.htm.

Senge, Peter M. (1990). The Leader's New Work: Building Learning Organizations, in *Sloan Management Review* (Fall 1990), pp. 7-23.

Saxenian, A. (2002). Transnational Communities and the Evolution of Global Production Networks: The Cases of Taiwan, China and India. Industry and Innovation, Special Issue on Global Production: 12.

Saxenian, AnnaLee. (2001). Bangalore: The Silicon Valley of Asia? Background paper, Conference on Indian Economic Prospects: Advancing Policy Reform. Center for Research on Economic Policy Reform, Stanford University.

Singhal, Arvind and Rogers, Everett M. (1989). India's Information Revolution. New Delhi: Sage Publications.

Sharma, Anurag. (2006). India's Ascent in IT and Infrastructure Woes. [online] http://www.smartindian.com/ITinfrastructure.htm

Shashi Tharoor. (1997). India: From Midnight to the Millennium. Viking Penguin New Delhi and Arcade Books, New York.

Sridharan, Eswaran. (1996). The Political Economy of Industrial Promotion: Indian, Brazilian, and Korean Electronics in Comparative Perspective 1969-1994. Praeger.

Srivastava, Siddharth. (2006). India Inc. on Global Company Buying Spree, Siliconeer, News Feature, Dated: Oct 13, 2006 [online] http://news.newamericamedia.org/news/view_article.html?article_id=951cea220715b28cc0adf1e5db8f49ad.

Sukumar, R. (2006). India's Best Employers: The Top 5. A BT-Hewitt study. Business Today. Retrieved on 2006-10-10.

US Department of Commerce. (2003). Education and Training for the Information Technology Workforce. Report to Congress from the Secretary of Commerce.

Waterstone, Richard. (1995). India: The Cultural Companion, Barnes and Noble, New York.

Wernerfelt, B. (1984) A Resource-Based View of the Firm, Strategic Management Journal, 5, 3, 171-180.

The World Bank. (2000). Higher Education in Developing Countries: Peril and Promise. The Task Force on Higher Education and Society. Washington, DC.

APPENDICES

Appendix A: Questions used in the Survey to guide this Research

1. What was your first interaction with someone from India?
2. What is your impression of India in the IT world?
3. Which year did India become noticeably competent in IT?
4. What is the major strength of India in IT?
5. What is the most distinct characteristic of Indian IT industry?
6. How do Indian IT companies differ from traditional Indian businesses?
7. How do Indian IT companies remain competitive and efficient?
8. What other areas besides IT, do you see India as an achiever in?
9. Can you name a few people responsible for India's IT success?
10. What are the challenges before Indian IT industry?
11. How is India dealing with these challenges?
12. Can India maintain its lead in IT for long? Why?
13. Can this success be replicated by other (developing/developed) nations? Why?
14. Can India imitate this success in other hi-tech areas e.g., biotech etc?
15. What role did government policies play in India's success in IT?
16. Why couldn't this success be predicted earlier?
17. How did Indian culture help or hinder the success in IT?
18. How is India balancing between traditional wisdom and cutting-edge technology?
19. Are under-privileged benefited by India's success in IT?
20. Is poverty reduced in India after IT revolution?

Appendix B: Policies that affected the Indian Software Industry

Year	Policy Action	Details
1972	Software Export Scheme	Hardware imports were permitted for purposes of software development on the condition that price of hardware was recouped through foreign exchange earnings within 5 years.
1976	Further liberalisation of policies related to the software industry	Hardware import duties reduced from over 100 % to 40 %; faster clearance of software export applications; software exporters could take advantage of export incentives including locating in EPZs; non-resident Indians allowed to import hardware for purposes of software export with a 100 % export obligation.
1981	Stricter controls on imports	Import duties on hardware were raised but firms were allowed to use hardware for development of domestic software as well as for exports; Software exporters could also import "loaned" computers.
1984	New Computer Policy	Import procedures for hardware-software simplified; import duties reduced from 135 % to 60 % for hardware and 100 % to 60 % for software; software recognised as an industry and licensing procedures simplified; improved access to foreign exchange for software firms; income tax exemption on net export earnings reduced from 100 % to 50 %
1986	Computer Software Export, Software Development and Training Policy	Imports of hardware & software were further de-regulated; anyone could import software at 60 % duty. 100 % export oriented software production units permitted to import hardware duty free; Indian firms allowed to sell foreign software, export obligations for hardware importers increased by 50 % and time in which to meet the obligations reduced to 4 years.
1988	STPI Scheme	Creation of software technology parks for production of software for export
1991	The Economy-wide Liberalisation Program	Devaluation and partial convertibility of the Rupee; abolition of foreign exchange for travel tax; reduction in telecommunications charges for satellite links; duty free and obligation free imports of telecommunications equipment in the STPs; reduction of import duties on software in 1994 to 20 % for applications software & 65% for systems software and in 1995 to 10 % for both; liberalisation of hardware import duties/loans for importing hardware given certain export obligations.
1992	Recent Tax Policies	Software exports brought under the Income Tax Act exempting exporters from income tax; confirmation of this status became open-ended in 1995. Software exports brought under the same chapter of the tax code as merchandise exports led to erosion of

| | | some of benefits due to the different characteristics between merchandise and software exports. Income tax exemption offered to EPZs and 100 per cent export oriented units was extended to software exports from companies taking part in these schemes which were established in or after 1993. |

Sources: Heeks (1996, pp. 42-49); Evans (1992); Sen (1995).

Appendix C: Acts related to Education in India

- The University Grants Commission Act, 1956

- National Commission on Education, 1964-66

- National Policy on Education, 1968

- National Policy on Education, 1986

- The All India Council for Technical Education Act, 1987

- Acharya Ramamurti Committee 1990.

- 1992 amendments to the National Policy on Education, 1986

- The National Council of Teacher Education Act, 1993

- The Persons with Disabilities (Equal Opportunities, Protection of Rights and Full Participation) Act, 1995

- The National Council for Minority Educational Institutions Act, 2004

Appendix D: Some Research Institutions in India

The Council of Scientific & Industrial Research (CSIR)
CSIR is the premier industrial R&D organization in India. It is the world's largest publicly funded R&D organization. It has linkages to academia, other R&D organizations and industry. It runs 40 research laboratories, two cooperative industrial research institutions and more than 100 extension and field centres making significant achievements.

Indian Space Research Organization (ISRO)
Under Department of Space (DoS), ISRO executes Space program through its various establishments in India. The prime objective of ISRO is to develop space technology and its application to various national tasks. ISRO has established two major space systems, INSAT for communication, television broadcasting and meteorological services, and Indian Remote Sensing Satellites (IRS) system for resources monitoring and management. ISRO has developed two satellite launch vehicles, PSLV and GSLV, to place INSAT and IRS satellites in the required orbits.

Tata Institute of Fundamental Research (TIFR)
Founded in 1945, TIFR may be considered as fountainhead of Indian IT. India's first computer TIFRAC was designed here.

Centre for the Development of Advanced Computing (C-DAC)
In 1991, C-DAC developed India's first supercomputer PARAM in record time when US sanctions made it impossible for India to acquire Cray supercomputer.

Computer Maintenance Corporation (CMC)
In 1998, when IBM left India after differences with the government, CMC came into existence primarily to take care of 800 odd IBM installations. CMC later developed INDONET, the first commercial computer network in India. CMC is now taken over by Tata Consultancy Services (TCS).

Electronic Corporation of India Limited (ECIL)
ECIL was established in 1967 under Atomic Energy commission and developed MEDHA which ran on its own operating system throughout 1970s. It nurtured some of the best engineers of India.

Bhabha Atomic Research Centre (BARC)
BARC is a premier research institution established in 1957. It covers entire spectrum of nuclear science, engineering, biotechnology and related areas.

Appendix E: State of some Advanced Technologies in India

Nanotechnology

Nanotechnology[102] is the engineering of functional systems at the molecular scale. It is an emerging technology which may provide practical solutions to many problems of today. With approximately 17 companies solely focussing in this are, India is not too far behind other developed countries.

Atomic Energy

India is today recognized as one of the most advanced countries in nuclear technology including production of source materials. US senate's approval of recent Indo-US nuclear cooperation agreement by a vote of 85 to 12 is clear indication of US recognition of India as a mature and equal nuclear partner.

Space Research

The Indian Space Research Organisation (ISRO), the Department of Space (DOS), National Remote Sensing Agency and Physical Research Laboratory are the main institutions in India to conducts research in the areas of satellite communications, remote sensing for resource survey, environmental monitoring, meteorological services, space science, and remote-sensing techniques for natural resource surveys and provides operational services to user agencies.

India is the only developing Country to develop its own remote-sensing satellite. India's progress in space technology has attracted worldwide attention and demand, with leasing agreements for marketing of IRS data and supply of space hardware and services. India also believes in co-operation in space with agencies all over the world. A high-level UN team selected India for setting up a UN Centre for Space Science and Technology Education. India is on the threshold of achieving self-reliance in the launch capability.

Oceanography

---

[102]Nanoscience is the study of the phenomena and manipulation of materials at atomic, molecular and macro-molecular scales where properties differ significantly from those at larger scale. Nanotechnology is the design, characterization, production, application and structure of this science

Since 1981, the Department of Ocean Development (DOD) conducts research in living and non-living resources such as hydrocarbons and minerals, and to harness ocean energy. DOD uses two research vessels, Sagar Kanya and Sagar Sampada besides several research laboratories. India has is a member of the elite group having a permanently manned base in Antarctica.

Bio-Technology
The advantage of low-cost economy and high-quality talent is making India emerge as a global hub for biotech too for the discovery and development of new drugs.

Department of Biotechnology (DBT), National Biotechnology Board, and the Biotechnology Consortium India Ltd are the institutions responsible for bio-technological research and its applications in increasing agricultural and industrial production, and in improving human and animal life. These organizations play the role of a catalyst in bridging the gap between research and development, industrial and financial institutions.

The Government has grants to the tune of Rs.5 million and loans to the tune of Rs.100 million at very low interest rates to scientists for drug discovery and development. Tax incentives and exemptions from the finance ministry are sought for drug manufacturing. Indian companies like Ranbaxy and Dr. Reddy's Lab have already become first generation multi-national drug companies while the later is emerging as the largest generic drug manufacturing company in the USA. Noida-based Jubilant has set up the Rs.750-million integrated, state-of-the-art drug discovery centre

Countries like USA and Canada have already started recognizing India's lead in this new hi-tech area. On December 5, 2006, Canada's Deputy Minister of Agriculture signed a pact with India's DBT to set up a knowledge city at Mohali in Punjab. A public-private enterprise, the park will have the National Agri-food Biotechnology Institute (NABI) and a bio-processing unit (BPU) to provide scale-up facilities.

Appendix F: Leadership that matters for Advancement of IT in India

Indira Gandhi

Indira Gandhi became the first woman prime minister of India in January 1966. In her leadership, India signed a 20-year friendship treaty of friendship with USSR in 1971 resulting in several scientific and hi-tech collaborations with a superpower. It helped India send its own cosmonaut in space besides other scientific achievements. She encouraged the research in advanced technology areas such as nuclear power, missile, rocket launching.

India conducted first underground nuclear test in 1974 during her regime. The green revolution and the white revolution both resulted in India's self sufficiency and even surplus in food and milk production. The Department of Ocean Development was established in 1981 to ensure optimum utilisation of living resources, exploitation of non-living resources such as hydrocarbons and minerals, and to harness ocean energy. During her time, India started scientific expeditions to Antarctica and established a permanent station there. She had a vision of a shining India and it was her period which strengthened Indian belief that India could be a very advanced country in near future.

Rajiv Gandhi

With eyes on 21st century, Rajiv Gandhi became prime minister of India in 1984. He announced a Computer Policy recognizing software as an industry and making it eligible for an investment allowance and other incentives. The policy also lowered import duties on software and personal computers (PCs) and permitted the import of computers in exchange for software exports at a special low duty.

He initiated the computerization of several government processes and systems including the gigantic Indian Railways reservation system. He created the Center for the Development of

Telematics (C-DoT) that pioneered indigenous digital switching technology to facilitate India's shift from electromechanical to digital switching and transmission.

Dr. N. Seshagiri

Additional Secretary at the Department of Electronics (DoE), Seshagiri had long argued that India's policies were too restrictive, its procedures too cumbersome, and the idea of self-reliance was self-defeating (Sridharan 1996). He believed that to become a major software exporter, India would have to begin with high volume, low-value-added exports and move up the value chain.

Satyanarayan Gangaram (Sam) Pitroda

He was invited by Mrs. Indira Gandhi to return to India to start the Center for Development of Telematics (C-Dot). He is considered responsible for the telecommunications revolution in India and specifically, the ubiquitous, yellow-signed Public Call Offices (PCO) that quickly brought cheap and easy domestic and international public telephones all over the country. Pitroda showed by action that adopting to the communication advancements was the need of the hour.

N. R. Narayana Murthy

In 1981, when N.R. Narayana Murthy founded Infosys (NASDAQ: INFY) with six other software professionals in Pune, very few people realized that he was going to be the driver of an unprecedented success wave that will sweep entire world. Today Infosys operates nine development centres in India and has over 30 offices worldwide. Annual revenues for fiscal year 2006 exceeded US$2.15 billion with a market capitalization of over US$30 billion. With over 66,000 employees worldwide, Infosys is one of India's largest IT companies. In 1999 Infosys attained a SEI-CMM Level 5 ranking and became the first Indian company to be listed on NASDAQ. In 2001 it was rated "Best Employer in India" by Business Today (Sukumar 2006) and in 2002 Business World (2004) named Infosys "India's Most Respected Company".

Narayana Murthy served as president of the National Association of Software and Service Companies, India from 1992 to 1994. In November 2006, Time magazine featured him in its list of "Asian Heroes". The list included 14 others with distinguished names such as Bill Gates, Steve Jobs and Warren Buffet. In December 2005, Narayana Murthy was voted as the 8th most admired CEO/Chairman in the world in a global study conducted by Burson-Marsteller with the Economist Intelligence Unit[103].

Chandrababu Naidu

Ex chief minister of the Indian state of Andhra Pradesh, Mr. Naidu was instrumental in making Hyderabad one of the IT hubs in the country. A key success to convince Microsoft set up its first Research Lab outside US in Hyderabad. He initiated an exercise to define "Vision 2020" for the state of Andhra Pradesh. He has been a vocal proponent of national policy reform. The National Task Force on Information Technology & Software Development was established in 1998 on his initiative. He pioneered the concept of "e-governance" in India. Institutions like International Institute of Information Technology, Hyderabad, Indian School of Business and Hi Tec City (which houses several IT companies) along with a modern administration can be construed to be his contribution to Andhra Pradesh, particularly, Hyderabad. While IT shone, agriculture paid the price. Farmers and weavers committed suicide as a routine during his tenure.

Dewang Mehta

Dewang Mehta was the head of NASSCOM from 1991 to 2001. He is credited with a large portion of India's momentous rise as a software "giant". Mehta's intensive parlays with the "right" people in the corridors of power, his cooperative stance with IT related departments and later with the Ministry of Communications & Information Technology (MCIT), enabled him to wrest concessions that other industries found hard to get through or match. Recognizing the potential of the software and services segment as a major foreign exchange earner, Mehta launched the India Inc. crusade, where he personally presented the country's software industry to the world.

---

[103]Rediff (URL: http://specials.rediff.com/money/2005/dec/15suman.htm)

ABOUT THE AUTHOR

Anurag Sharma

Anurag Sharma grew up in the historical town of Bareilly, India. He earned a bachelor's degree in Mathematics, Physics, and Chemistry from MJRP University, India. He also holds a master's degree in Information Technology and Management from Sheffield Hallam University, UK. A Microsoft Certified Professional, Anurag is an Information Architect by profession. He is a published poet and a story writer too. He got inspiration to write from his grandfather who was a Second World War veteran besides being a Sanskrit and Farsi scholar. He founded PittRadio – an online Indian radio from Pittsburgh.